		DATE DUE	

D0558580

Provides practical guidelines and a
straightforward approach as to how
restitution can be implemented in the
classroom and schools.

To order copies of *It's All About We: Rethinking
Discipline Using Restitution* contact
Chelsom Consultants Limited
134 110th Street, Saskatoon, SK S7N 1S2
www.realrestitution.com
1-800-450-4352

TABLE OF CONTENTS

Acknowledgements   7

Introduction   9

Chapter One - Is It Okay To Coerce?   13

Contingent On Your Compliance   15
What Gives Us The Right?   18
Cultural Differences   19
Why Do People Behave?   21
Change The Way You Think About It!   23
Restitution Self Discipline is Rooted in Aboriginal Practices   27
The Restitution Triangle   33
Summary Questions   36

Chapter Two – Our Journey   37

What are the Five Positions of Control?   38
What is Punishment? Are You a Punisher?   47
Responsibility: What Does It Really Mean?   50
What Is Monitoring?   51
Be a Buddy and Catch Them Being Good!   53
What is a Positive Environment?   54
What is Planning?   55
What is the Difference Between a Consequence and a Restitution?   57
Why is My Job/Your Job Not Enough?   59
What is Weaving Between the Monitor and the Manager?   64
Summary – Monitor-Manager Assessment   70

Chapter Three – Shoulder to Shoulder   71

Restitution is Not a Payback; It is a Pay Forward   73
Restitution Restores Relationships   80
Restitution is an Invitation Not Coercion   81
Restitution Teaches the Person to Look Inside   84
Restitution is About Looking For the Basic Need Behind the Problem   87
Self Restitution is the Most Powerful Tool   93
Restitution is about "Being" Not "Doing"   95
Restitution Strengthens   97
Restitution Focuses on Solutions   102
Restitution Restores One to the Group   107
Summary – What Is A Good Restitution?   112

Chapter Four – Developing the Moral Sense   **113**

How Does the Brain Work?   114
The Brain is Social   118
Why Do They Say What They Say?   121
Why Would We Care About How Our Brain Works?   123
Ask, Don't Tell   128
Are You Ready For the Challenge?   131
Summary Questions and Answers   134

Chapter Five – It's a Pull System, Not a Push System   **135**

Why Have Beliefs? Why Not Just Have Rules?   135
How to Establish the Social Contract   139
Pitfalls of the Social Contract: Mixing Beliefs and Rules   141
A Process For Staff Beliefs   146
How to Keep the Social Contract Alive   148
Summary of Beliefs   149
Bottom Lines Protect Beliefs   150
Administration and Bottom Lines   153
Examples of Bottom Lines   156
From Old Think To New Think   160
Summary of Bottom Lines   164
Appreciation to Restitution Schools   165

APPENDIX – Restitution Schools Report   **169**

Elementary Schools   169
Middle Schools   174
High Schools   185
District Wide Change   188

Resources   **218**

For my loving mother Elinor,

a teacher who models life long learning.

Acknowledgements

Without the assistance of my colleague Dr. Judy Anderson this book would not have been written. She read and revised as well as contributed a major section on the Social Contract. I thank Laurel Chelsom and Lila McCormick and Elinor Stinson for their contribution as editors. Jackie Eaton who runs my business with enthusiasm and competence contributed her patience and skill in compiling *It's All About We*. I thank Lindsay Boychuk for all the speedy typing she has done. Over the years I have gained wisdom in conversations with Esther Sanderson and Jeremiah McLeod, my Aboriginal friends. Yves Bousquet, with his community leadership in Saskatchewan has been a source of strength to me. The generosity of these three has helped to shape my understanding. Your time has been a gift to me.

For twenty-five years I had the opportunity to learn from Dr. William Glasser as a faculty member of his organization. He is a pioneer in helping schools become all they can be. William Powers, the founder of Perceptual Control Theory, is the finest teacher I have ever had. His hierarchy of perceptions opened my eyes to a new way of viewing human behavior. Finally I wish to express my appreciation to the Restitution Facilitators and Trainers as well as the parents, staff and students who have pioneered these ideas. From Inuvik in the Arctic to Princess Alexandra Community School in my home town, from Eagan-Apple Valley to Reyjavik, from Vancouver to Watertown and from Zagreb to Sydney we have been on a journey. You have taught me more than I have taught you and I am grateful.

Diane Gossen
Saskatoon, Saskatchewan 2004

Introduction

"I've worked in this district a dozen years and I've had more profound conversations with all sorts of people in the month since the introductory Restitution workshop than I've had in the last decade." "What kind of conversations are you having?" I asked. The person who had hired me said, "People are really reflecting on what they want to be in the lives of the children. They are also having insights into their personal relationships with family members and friends. They are challenging themselves to be less coercive and to help the students want to learn for the love of learning. When they hear themselves using a guilting or criticizing tone they are trying so hard to change and to tell the youth their intent. When they do, the road is opening up into the soul of the child."

A father in one of the parent groups said, "These ideas have changed the way I look at my children as human beings. I am not the same person I was when we started these classes. I have such gratitude for this learning." When people have made the paradigm shift in discipline they talk about how they are changing what they do rather than talking about how those around them won't change. When the shift takes place teachers will ask different questions. First we will ask them of ourselves.

Another conversation I had the same day was with a friend who told me she had cried that morning in her car with gratitude. Her son had had a very bad bout with drugs and his recovery had taken two years. Now she was celebrating the completion of his studies and his full return to the person she knew and loved. I reminded her how patient she had been with him, how she had reduced her expectations but kept her optimism, and how courageous she had been to confront his problem. I know how hard she had worked to hold her tongue, to see his point of view and to support small changes in hundreds of concrete ways. In a very uncontrollable situation, she had made a strong picture of who she wanted to be and she had stayed on the course, evaluating herself and encouraging him to do the same.

You may ask why I am beginning a book on Restitution Self Discipline with such personal examples, what has this to do with having reduced incidents of discipline and orderly learning? I start at this point for two reasons. First because I want to model the importance of personalizing the learning, and secondly you have the right to know your author, who I am, where I have come from and how I have learned from my teachers in life. My friends tease me, they say "You made up the idea of Restitution because you make so many mistakes!" I smile and agree my life has been two steps forward and one step back. I have learned to use one step back as an opportunity to self evaluate and learn rather than to criticize myself. As Oprah says "We did the best with what we knew; now we know more so we can do better."

When I first went teaching I taught a grade eight class. I had a fifteen-year-old student in my class who came reluctantly because he was on probation. I can still see his face, his lanky frame and his curly hair. He lounged in the back of the class refusing to work. I was twenty years old and thought my job was to make him do his work. I cajoled and when that didn't work I warned him, and then gave ultimatums. Push came to shove and because this was a very long time ago, the policy of the school was to give the student a strap on the hand with a belt in order to gain his compliance. I had no more trouble with him after the principal did that. Joe did his work, but he never looked me in the eye the rest of the year. I guess in a way I temporarily solved my problem, but as I think back I feel ashamed at the person I was with him.

Here was a boy, possibly in his last year of education. Legally he didn't have to return and I'm sure he didn't. What had I offered him for understanding, for learning? Had I been the person I want to be with Joe? My shame and regret today say no that I had not. However, at age twenty I didn't even know how to look inside and to evaluate my own behavior. I am sure I dealt with my discomfort by displacing balance on Joe rather than assuming responsibility for myself. Why? Because I didn't know any better. I was evaluating my success by the actions of those around me. I was not asking myself what kind of teacher I wanted to be or what kind of human being I wanted to grow in my classroom.

As a young wife, I was sad in my first year of marriage because I wanted my husband to be different to me – more communicative like my own family. I worked very hard to change him and in retrospect I know I did not help him. How much better it would have been if I had asked myself what would a generous, understanding, supporting, loving and playful spouse be doing. If I had done that I could have grown myself and also the relationship.

What Is It I Wish I Had Known?

I wish at twenty I had understood that people have different pictures of how things should be. Now I know the importance of building common pictures together. If I had practised this at home and created an ideal class concept with my students, there would have been a place for everyone. I wish I had stayed in self evaluation making self restitution to my family and students rather than coercing them. I wish I had understood then that the only person I can control is myself. How much better it would have been if I had looked down the road and asked myself who I wanted to be in the life of this person rather than focusing on changing others.

I am writing this book for two reasons. The first is to celebrate the outstanding efforts of colleagues, teachers and parents who have taken the theory of Restitution and implemented it in their lives, with their schools and with their families. The second is to answer as many questions as I can that have been posed to me by people who are involved in making a genuine paradigm shift from external discipline which coerces and alienates youth to internal discipline which strengthens and embraces youth. I am very excited to review the past ten years of Restitution practices and to share with you what we have learned in the field.

CHAPTER ONE

IS IT OK TO COERCE?

*We must come together in ways that respect the solitude of the soul, that avoid
the unconscious violence we do when we try to save each other, that evoke our
capacity to hold another life without dishonoring it's mystery, never trying to
coerce the other into meeting our own needs.* -- Parker J. Palmer

"Is it okay to coerce people for their own good? What will they remember
years after – their success or the feeling of being coerced?" I have had two
experiences that caused me to reflect on this. The first was a conversation
with a former staff member from Radius, the longest, continuously running
Reality Therapy based program in the world.   Several years ago we had a
staff reunion. On this occasion a former teacher remarked to me "When you
were my director I loved you and I hated you." I was a bit caught off guard
and asked, "Why would you say that?" She responded "Well you always
thought I could do more than I thought I could do. I said to her "Well you
did it didn't you?" She said "Yes, but it was so uncomfortable." The next
day I seriously reflected on this. I remembered that I often asked her to take
on the more difficult students because she had had a rough upbringing
herself and I knew she could relate to them. Sometimes she deferred saying
she was overloaded with aggressive kids. I believe that at this point I
praised her, extolling her skills. If she demurred again I would say "If you
don't take him who's going to help him?" At this point because of guilt she
complied with my request. She was always successful but 30 years later she
remembers "feeling uncomfortable."

I also thought about the question of coercion when I was asked by a childcare worker in Quebec, "Is it okay to force the kids in the halfway houses to do 'on the job training'? You know it strengthens them." I answered, "You're right but the question is what will they remember - their success in the program or the fact that they were forced to participate?"

Now I ask you. How many of you reading this book was forced to practise a musical instrument or to play a sport? Did having to attend church or temple make you a spiritual person? Can you think of a time that you complied, but dropped an activity as soon as the pressure was off? Were you forced to dress or act a certain way, but changed as soon as you were out of sight? Think of a recent time you showed affection? Did you do so to avoid a conflict or did you do it because you felt it. The act is the same. The result is very different.

In working with a new group each week over the past year, I have plenty of opportunities to hear their answers to these questions. A common response is "Yes, it's okay to coerce for safety, such as preventing a small child from going on the road." People feel age is a factor and that youth don't understand the possible consequences of their actions. People also speak of the need to exert force if someone is going to hurt him or herself or another. On the other hand, there are very diverse opinions about practicing the piano. Many report they were made to practise. Some are grateful; others never touch the piano today. One person reports loving to play another instrument now but not the piano. Several express the wish that their parents had forced them to practise. How about you?

Who decides what is good for another? Who really knows? Whose needs are being met? Let me ask you "What really is coercion?" If we define it as pressure it can be positive or negative. People ask, "What's the difference between encouraging and persuading?" or "Where is the line between guiding and coercing?" or "What is challenging and what is forcing?" "Inspiration and motivation…when do they become coercion?" "What's the difference between a gift and a bribe?" "Is daring a person to do something coercive?" When I ask, "Do you have a feeling that tells you when you are being coerced?" people nod vigorously in affirmation and answer, "When we feel we have no choice."

Some groups take a global view. One group said the conformity of communism was comfortable for people in Russia but the price was freedom and independence. Another said that Japan is stronger on conformity than on creativity. North American Native Indian participants express their view that it is disrespectful to pressure a person. They even espouse a principle of non-interference to give people a chance to make-up their own minds. Someone said "We can coerce people in Iraq but the minute we leave they'll go back to being the way they want to be."

CONTINGENT ON YOUR COMPLIANCE?

The second big question asked is from the work of Alfie Kohn, "Is it okay to take what people want and need and make the receipt of it contingent on their compliance?" What does it do to the relationship? I ask you as you read this to think about your friendships and your intimate relationships. Would your friends still be your friends if you withheld approval from them in order to control them? What would happen if your loved one withheld the affection which you need in order to get you to do something for him or her? Does coercing a person to comply show our lack of optimism and belief in their innate goodness, in their deep desire to love and to learn, and in their internal motivation to achieve?

Do we let ourselves be more coerced by those we admire? Can we avoid being influenced by those we love? Is it easy to resist coercion if you have no respect for the person who uses it? One person said, "My mother did everything for me. It was a burden after awhile. I left home to rebel. I didn't even leave a phone number." Another asks, "Do people say, thanks for making me do that?" What about marriage? Does a person choose marriage for rules and consequences? Do you say, "Let's get married so we can control each other?" Do you accept a job for the joy of being monitored and rewarded? Why do you choose your profession and who do you want to be? A lot of people say coercion is part of life so just get used to it. Many note that the education system is based on coercion. Others feel any organization has the right to coerce an individual.

Sometimes in my workshops I say a compliment feels good the first time and okay the second time. Then I ask, "How does it feel the third time?" and everyone intones, "What do they want from me?" It's not the compliment that is a problem. It is our habit of giving compliments to induce others to behave in a certain manner to meet our own needs not their needs.

It is not bubble gum itself that is the problem, nor money, nor love and attention. The rewards themselves are in some cases innocuous

16   *Is Okay To Coerce?*

and in other cases indispensable. What concerns me is the practice of using these things as rewards. To take what people want or need and offer it on a contingent basis in order to control how they act— this is where the trouble lies.[1]

This is not to suggest that we stop expressing pleasure to others. If a compliment is heartfelt and spontaneous it does not have a dangerous side. Our pleasure may also be revealed non-verbally with a nod or a hug. It is important to cue people to the impact of their actions on us. They can then decide how to behave in relation to us. If our delight is genuine and an integrated part of our behavior our goal is not coercion.

Unfortunately, the legacy of stimulus response teaching has urged us to synthesize and to simulate pleasure in order to impact on others in an attempt to control them. Particularly this is true with regard to children. I could pull off my shelf at random a dozen books on education and self-help from my shelf at random. If they were written in the last half of the 20th century there is a good chance they will contain a section on positive reinforcement. Parents will be encouraged to mete out praise. Teachers will be exhorted to single out high performers for recognition. Lovers are encouraged to do acts of service to gain their partners approval. Behavior problems will be dealt with by rewarding people for being good. The examples are endless.

This can also be depicted within any teen magazine for girls. Such titles as *Seventeen* urge them to adopt certain wiles to attract the opposite sex. To be honest, I can remember having similar conversations with my daughters

---

[1] Alfie Kohn, *Punished By Rewards*, Boston: Houghton Mifflin Company, 1993, p.4.

when they were dating advising them how to attract someone such as giving compliments and feigning interest in what they liked. However, now I would say, "Be the person you want to be and see who loves you." Otherwise what happens is people seeking dates package themselves to please the object of their affection. As the relationship progresses their true self will eventually be revealed. When this occurs their partner will feel disappointed that they are not what they seemed to be and the relationship breaks down.

If people are in touch with who they really are they may attract fewer people initially, but those they attract will stay because of the authenticity of the first contact. I had a conversation with my niece last year in which she revealed that she had gone through a conflict in her junior year as to whether she should be what others wanted her to be or be herself. She chose the latter and reported that she had even more friends and as a result of being genuine was chosen class president. Whether we're talking about a marriage, a friendship, or a teacher/student relationship, unless the individual we engage feels free and has independence, they will gravitate away from us to other settings that offer more freedom.

WHAT GIVES US THE RIGHT?

This brings us to reflect on another basic principle. What gives us the right to evaluate another person's behavior? Why do we think it is our responsibility? Have we considered that any evaluation may be disruptive? I have noticed that even when I am giving a person a positive observation, that comment disrupts their focus. As they continue their task they now have two things to pay attention to - the initial goal and my opinion of their performance. They may even be distracted from a creative choice in order to provide me with more of what I want to see. This was especially true if I was a significant other and in a position of authority.

I have not even touched on the concept of rewards. Much has been written on this. It is not only the rewards themselves that pose a problem, but the fact that we withhold them to assert influence. I have a saying, "We make the place for them to feel bad." How do we do this? By accustoming them to a certain level of reward or praise or even encouragement then suddenly removing it. My brother opens a present and smiles and everyone knows he likes it. I open a present, smile and say something about the present that I like or how I plan to use it. My sister opens a present and if she doesn't say she loves it three times we say to her "What's wrong?" She has accustomed us to that level of positive response. How is it in your family? What about the family you married into? Is there a difference for men and women? Is there a geographic difference? A cultural difference?

CULTURAL DIFFERENCES

I noticed a big difference between Maine and North Carolina when I worked in these states. Positive reinforcement was not so common in Maine as in North Carolina. A Japanese-born woman who married an American sailor and moved to Seattle told me the most difficult thing for her to learn was to give compliments. She said she felt it was disrespectful to comment on another person's performance, but forced herself to do it so they would know their hospitality to her was appreciated. Another example I can think of is when nine Australians attended an International Conference in Los Angeles. The conference was three days long so they designated three persons each day to give compliments so the hosts would know they admired their efforts. They told me that the need for such reinforcement was necessary in America, but would be considered "over the top" in Australia, making their task uncomfortable.

My friend who comes from Norwegian Lutheran stock also provided me with insight. She told me compliments were very rare in her family because of the emphasis on personal humility. She said that when she and her siblings did well, it was viewed as doing what was expected. Therefore, there was no need for a comment. However, when a performance was not up to par, they experienced a silence sometimes laced with guilt or disappointment. How was it for you?

My husband's family was Scottish. He never heard compliments and was not expected to give them. When I married him I expected lots of positive reinforcement because it was how I had been raised. When I didn't hear it, I felt pain. I even felt unloved. When I hinted for it, I'm sure at least half the time my spouse missed the cue. The other half he may have felt coerced to do something that was not natural to him. I was only nineteen. I didn't know better.

Why do we do what we do? An interesting question. We try to receive input from the world that matches the expectation we set for ourselves. Different cultural filters result in different expectations. In one culture commenting on a person is considered ill mannered. In another, the same behavior is interpreted as concern. In another, such commentary is a gauntlet thrown down for a verbal duel challenging us to marshal our defenses. It is not so much what we say or do but why we say or do it that needs to be examined to gain self-understanding.

WHY DO PEOPLE BEHAVE?

Every time something is not the way we want it to be, we behave to change it. How do we behave? We act, we think and we feel and our body responds. Why do we behave? This is a more difficult question. Do we behave because forces in our environment shape us? Sometimes we seem to behave to avoid pain, but if we didn't care about safety we might not notice pain. Why else might someone behave? Well, we seem to behave to get something we want. Do you agree? Do you behave to get a smile, a paycheck, a reward? Why else might a person behave? James Wilson in *The Moral Sense* suggests these three reasons.

Three Reasons People Behave

Level One – To avoid pain

Level Two – For respect or reward from one another

Level Three – For respect of self

You can identify where each person is behaving by the questions they ask. If they ask, "What happens if I don't do it?" they are behaving to avoid pain due to the disruption of a need, physical or psychological. If they ask, "What do I get if I do it?" They are behaving to gain approval or reward from those significant others they have placed in their quality world. If they ask, "Who will I be if I do it?" they are behaving to become the person they aspire to be, for respect of self.

Have you ever been in a situation where you deliberately did something that actually caused you pain or interfered with approval or reward from others? Have you spoken out in favor of an unpopular cause or defended someone under attack? Why would you do this if the result appears to be pain, social censure or perhaps financial loss? Why did you behave thusly? What belief were you protecting? What kind of person were you being? Think about yourself. You are reading this book right now. Why are you reading it? Are you reading it because something unpleasant could happen if you don't? Perhaps you could be called upon to summarize its contents. Are you behaving because a significant other has asked you to read it and you wanted to please that person? Perhaps you will look good if you can quote recent literature. Or, are you reading this for yourself? Are you reading to evaluate whether it will be useful in helping you become the teacher, parent, friend or person you want to become?

Stop and self evaluate for a minute. Perhaps your motivation for reading this is a combination of all three reasons we behave. It would not be unusual to behave initially to avoid discomfort, then to see how doing it could have a pay off. Finally you could be engaged in quality understanding, as you see how an idea can be useful and exciting to your becoming the person you want to be.

What is your family belief? What do you believe? What does it say about you if you do it? Will it help you to be loving, powerful, free, and playful? Why would you want to do this? Who are you becoming?

CHANGE THE WAY YOU THINK ABOUT IT!

If you want to change an unpleasant chore for yourself, experiment with shifting your perception. If you go to an event you are dreading, decide in advance if you are going to do it to avoid discomfort, to please someone else or because you are being the person you want to be - caring, responsible, committed. An onerous social occasion, a bottle drive for your young child, or a visit to a senior citizens' home or studying for exams to please your parents can take on new significance. If you tie it to the approval of any of the recipients you will be bereft and at a loss if they do not thank you. If you do it just to avoid pain you will feel an energy leak manifest as fatigue or resentment. If you do it to be the person you want to be you will be energized and fulfilled. The time expended will be exactly the same. The experience can be significantly different. Only in the final position will you gain internal strength.

I had an aunt I visited at the old folk's home. I had been feeling guilty saying, to myself, "I should go and visit her." I went to avoid pain (Level One). Sometimes I'd go because I thought she'd be happy to see me. But she didn't always recognize me. So when I went for her approval and she didn't recognize me, I felt bereft. I thought, "Why did I make the effort. It doesn't make a difference to her. There's no payoff in it for me (Level Two)!

I intentionally tried to shift my thinking to the third level. I asked myself, what do we believe in our family about taking care of older people? How do

I want to be treated when I am this age? What does it say about me if I care for her? Who will I be if I do it? This is internal motivation.

By moving myself to the third level, I was able to self evaluate at the highest level of moral reasoning and I always felt satisfied. I noticed I stopped telling people I was going to visit her as if I had been doing it to avoid their censure. If she was asleep I just sat with her and didn't feel disappointed because my satisfaction was not dependent on her acceptance of my gesture. I was doing it for myself, to strengthen myself and to grow.

Another example occurred on the night several years ago when I phoned home and spoke to my spouse. In response to my "What are you doing?" he answered, "I'm watering your plants" and he said it in a begrudging tone so I suspected he was doing it to avoid pain (Level One). A sweeter tone to me might have indicated he was doing it to please me (Level Two). This position might have been all right for him as long as I expressed appreciation to him for his efforts. If not he would feel ripped off. That's the problem with Level Two, the need for respect or reward from others. This level requires dependence on the other's response to feel good. My response to him was, "Why don't you do it for yourself, you like the plants." (Level Three). When I got home I asked him one other question, "Did you think about what I said about the plants?" He said, "It wasn't as significant to me as it was to you." Hmmm.

When I had returned home on another occasion, my son had said, "Mom you check the plants even before you said 'Hi' to me," and he was right! What do you think I found when I checked the plants? Dry? No, soaking wet.

And when had they been watered? Probably as I was being driven from the airport. And how do you think my son was feeling? Resentment? Fear? Guilt? Probably some negative feeling because that is the legacy of doing things from the Level I position. It's remotely possible he might have been joyously watering, but I doubt it based on the dry buds in the pots.

To finish this story I want to say that after that brief conversation with my spouse, the plants started to look better. When I came home they were damp, not wet and when we moved the gardenia tree to the front porch my spouse had said, "Don't put it there, it doesn't like that much light." Now was he resonating with them, playing them music, talking to them? I doubt it, but I'll bet the feeling he had was more satisfying as the plants were being watered. It took him the same amount of time but the result was strengthening rather than being an energy leak.

I have a friend who when she heard teachings about the three reasons people behave, recognized that she dreaded making supper. She said she was going into the grocery store and slamming food into the cart. She knew when there was a bad feeling she was doing it to avoid pain. So she said she sat in the parking lot before she went into the store and asked herself, "Why do I want to make this supper anyway?" I could buy it or I could let everyone make their own. Next she thought, "I could do this to please them, for the family." Then she thought that if they didn't say thanks she'd feel unsatisfied because she would be doing it for the reward. Then she asked herself, "Why is it important to me for the family to have supper together? Why is it important to make it with my own hands?" She answered herself from her core beliefs. She had heard that a family who always ate supper together stayed together and she had wanted this picture for herself. Now when she goes to the grocery store instead of experiencing anger she feels with every item she puts in her grocery cart that she is being more of the wife and mother she wants to be. So instead of her energy being depleted she is strengthening herself.

Choose something you are dreading doing in the next week and stop now and think about why you are dreading it. If you are dreading it, it is likely to avoid pain, Level One! Try now to move yourself to Level Three by reflecting on your beliefs. You may find Level Three encompasses Level Two. For example, the person I want to be is also a person who helps others meet their needs. Level Three is not a selfish position. Think about an onerous social engagement, a demanding activity with a child, a clean up or organizing job or confronting a difficult situation. See if you can feel the shift in motivation and energy!

What Do The People In Your Life Say

To Avoid Pain.

What will happen if I don't do it?

For respect or reward from others.

What do I get if I do it?

Respect from self.

Who will I be if I do it?

QUESTIONS TO THINK ABOUT:

1. Think of something you were forced to do as a child. How did you feel? What has been the long term result?

2. Think of a friend or spouse. Have they tried to coerce you to do what they want? How did they do it – positive or negative pressure? What was the outcome for you?

3. Think of something you want to change in another person. What influence are you using: persuasion, silence, disapproval, rewards, consequences? Why do you do this? Do you have or not have confidence in the inner wisdom of this other person?

4. Think of something you love to do. How did you learn it? How does it feel to do it?

RESTITUTION SELF DISCIPLINE IS ROOTED IN ABORIGINAL PRACTICES

Much of what I learned and put into Restitution Self Discipline is rooted in Aboriginal practices. Independence is encouraged rather than conformity. There is a strong group built by the adults and children through shared beliefs. Elder Bill McLean of the Stony People talked about traditional child rearing. He said that when he was in residential school and the supervisors tried to scare kids into compliance he told me there were always some students who would not give in, even if they were punished because deep inside they knew it was not the right thing to do. They were very courageous and strong in their values at a young age. They could not be bullied or threatened into hurting another person. They were behaving to be the person they wanted to be.

Ernie Phillips who is an elder at Salmon Arm, BC came to their Restitution training. He asked to speak. He talked about how he was hurt as a child when he went to school and how he learned to hate white people. As a man he healed himself and now is back to his early view of being connected with all human beings. Many of you reading this have heard similar stories. Western discipline based on punishment does not strengthen youth. It shames them and weakens their resolve to do the right thing. It alienated them. Punishment is aimed at breaking the group apart rather than using the strength of the group for healing.

People sometimes look at a child, a loved one, a street person, or even a politician and say, "He is bad." As we become more educated we learn to say, "His behavior is bad," judging not the individual but his acts. Psychology classes teach us to separate the person from his behavior, but they never question the wisdom of judging what he does. Aboriginal people learn something different. They learn that it is disrespectful to evaluate others. One can only give information about how one feels. They choose not to identify the source of the problem with the person but rather to own responsibility for it. If you ask an elder to comment on a community the worst thing they would ever say is that the people are having a hard time helping each other.

The Principle of Non-interference

Many a time I have heard an Aboriginal person say, "I'm not going back because it doesn't feel good there." They act for themselves and they are taught that it is undesirable to draw conclusions about another's motives. Sometimes we misread this as indifference when parents confronted with their child's behavior say, "It's up to him" rather than passing judgment. This is the respectful principle of non-interference with another's behavior. Rupert Ross says, "I have come to see traditional child rearing as a three-legged stool, where two of the legs, teaching children responsibilities [to the group] and developing their personal attributes and skills, made it possible to allow for a third leg of almost complete independence to make particular choices."[2] Justice Rupert Ross, a Canadian judge was funded to travel Northern Canada for two years to study First Nations Justice practices. The principle of non-interference works well in a stable respectful society where children look around and see adults exemplifying their values. It doesn't work in a society where television is a stronger teacher than the family or where adults are abusive and not helping by modeling their values. As tribal communities are impacted by the major society it becomes harder to retain these principles. Martin Brokenleg and Larry Brendtro[3] Reclaiming Youth Seminars do a very good job teaching First Nations beliefs to work with troubled youth.

---

[2] Rupert Ross, *Returning To The Teachings*, Toronto: Penguin Books 1996, p.84.
[3] Larry Brendtro, Martin Brokenleg and Steve Van Bockern. *Reclaiming Youth At Risk: Our Hope for the Future.* Bloomington: National Educational Service, 1990.

The Concept of Blame

The concept of blame in Aboriginal culture differs from that of European culture. In the non Aboriginal culture forgiveness involves an initial supposition that the offender should have been responsible and not done harm. Among native people, because they don't seek to find fault in the first place there is no need to forgive. Acceptance of human frailty is a basic premise. A person's offense is viewed as the result of outside forces not always under control. This view is not to promote excuse making or to excuse the person from responsibility. It is however consistent with a view of behavior which advocates looking at the whole person, not just his/her offense. We need to look at what's going on in the environment and community and ask, "What are the outside influencing factors?" Do the youth have easy access to alcohol? Have the sports facilities been closed down? Does this person have family to help them?

Ross gives us these words from the Sandy Lake Band of North Western Ontario:

> Probably one of the most serious gaps in the system is the different perception of wrongdoing and how to treat it. In the non-Native society, committing a crime seems to mean that the individual is a bad person and must be punished... The Indian communities view wrongdoing as a misbehavior which requires teaching or an illness which requires healing.[4]

My friend raised on The Pas Reserve in Manitoba, helped me learn this concept. I asked her how she was disciplined as a child. I knew her mother didn't speak English, only Cree. She said what I have heard from other

---

[4] Rupert Ross, *Dancing With A Ghost*, 1992, p. 62.

Aboriginal people, "It's hard to find the words in English." When pressed she said, "The direct translation would be, the right thing you're not doing it. I asked if she meant right as in right or wrong. She said, "No, the right thing meaning the moral thing, the way of our people." Then I asked her if the adults told her what to do to fix her mistake. She said, "They never told us. We had to look around and figure it out for ourselves." I said, "What if your snowshoes were on backwards, did they say they were on the wrong way?" She said, "They'd say that they're on backwards then we would have to decide what to do." Then I asked her what her grandmother would do if she spilled something. My friend said "She'd just throw me a rag." Then she said "No, if my Kookum thought I could fix it on my own she would pretend not to notice because it was too embarrassing for me."

How different I thought from how most of us had been raised. Our mistakes would have been pointed out to us maybe with impatience, but more likely with a light guilt. Our parents and I myself thought it was our duty to correct the children in our family. Mistakes were seen as bad. They were not viewed as opportunities to learn and to correct oneself. We thought children had to be made to fix things. We didn't understand that everyone has the desire to make things right if given a chance.

When in 1978 I worked for Brandon University in Northern Manitoba at Cross Lake, Island Lake, and Oxford House, I was impressed by the dignity of the five year old children who came to school. They had no television at this time. They had little English and they had been raised in a traditional manner to be independent and to think of the effect of their actions on others. When I sat in the one room airport toddlers were not whining, having tantrums or banging on the candy machine. They were calm. Their needs were met. They observed and they were patient. When in Cross Lake I observed in Jennifer Thompson's room as she taught them in Cree, the primary children listened and wanted to cooperate with each other. They were very self-disciplined. I started to pay attention and to learn this way of working with children. Many of the ideas in my book *Restitution: Restructuring School Discipline* were learned through these teachings. For example I included the story from Island Lake of Peter who was independently drawing until a teacher from down south inadvertently created a dependence by complimenting him. When she commented on his picture he first looked surprised then looked pleased because the teacher was an important person who smiled at him. The next day he began to watch for the teacher and to hold up his picture for praise. His independence had shifted to dependence. Then when he didn't want to draw and she withdrew her praise he experienced a loss. He behaved in a variety of ways. Sometimes he started drawing to please her. Sometimes he scrunched up his paper. Other times he put his head down and wouldn't work. Each time he was looking outside for the teacher's response rather than inside for the joy of drawing. In one week he had gone from an internal to an external focus.

I asked myself, "What right had I to evaluate another, either positively or negatively?" Was it true that positive comments disrupted a person's locus of control? I wondered if I had an obligation to comment on others as a parent, teacher, and counselor. Could compliments interfere with another's autonomy? Could compliments deprive others of ownership of their achievements? If so, in what way would this happen? How could I give information and own it as only as my perception? What gives me the right

Is It Okay To Coerce?

to comment on others? Would it be called arrogance or would it be named caring to do so? I told myself to think about the result of my comments long after the conversation was over.

The main difference I observed was that Aboriginal people asked children to look inside to know if they were doing the right thing. When I asked an elder, "Am I doing the right thing?" she would say, "Look inside yourself and you will know the answer." My culture taught children to look outside for rewards or to avoid consequences. Aboriginal values taught independent thinking and self-discipline. When Louis Bear was sent to the residential school his grandfather told him, "Never forget who you are and don't let you feelings be a problem to other people." In the schools in which I was raised children had to be supervised all the time to see if they were meeting expectations. The teachers were responsible for discipline and students would behave only when they were there to monitor them.

THE RESTITUTION TRIANGLE

The Restitution Triangle process which you will recognize throughout this book reflects the concepts I observed in Aboriginal culture as well as the ideas of Control Theory and Reality Therapy. Restitution Self-Discipline focuses on using the Restitution Triangle. On Side I of the triangle we stabilize the youth moving him or her from fear and anger and failure so that learning can take place. From Aboriginal culture I learned to focus on safety and learning. We say, "It's okay to make a mistake. You're not the only one. Your mistake is a small part of a big life. We want you to be part of our group. We can solve this together. You are not alone. "

Side II of the Restitution embodies the "Art of Restitution". It is based on the principles that at any given moment, given the context and given the way one is perceiving the world, a person is doing the best he or she can. The corollaries to this thesis are two: 1) the person didn't choose the worst possible choice for themselves at the moment and 2) the person could be doing worse. It also follows that if there is a worse option there may also be a better one. We explore two worst options to discover what the person could have done that would have been either more aggressive or what the person could have done that would have been more passive (usually inaction or not caring). This process will be covered in detail further on in this book. Let me share a common example: If a youth is teased about his family and fights back, the worst option for him would be to not care about protecting his family. Not caring is the more passive option he is avoiding. Fighting is his aggressive choice. What would be more aggressive would be to fight with us and to not listen. We can ensure this will happen if we castigate him. If we ask, "Could you have done worse?" we engage the youth and he can begin to understand his motivation. We can validate his family loyalty and ask him to stick up for himself without violence. If a child lies or cheats we would term this as a passive behavior because it involves hiding, secretive behavior. What do you think would be the worse thing the child is avoiding? Most likely failure and punishment. Could he be doing worse? A more passive option would be to not care about coming to school at all. A more aggressive option would be to rip up the paper and tell the teacher to "f"-off! Always the answer to "Could you have done worse?" is "Yes, not meet my needs."

Side III of the Restitution Triangle taps internal ideal pictures and shared values on this side. We ask the youth, "Think about the kind of person you want to be". We also refer to the agreements the group has made. These may be family, class or team beliefs. It is crucial that our questions here are in a calm tone rather than being guilting or confrontational. The goal is for the youth to tap his or her moral sense. You may have done work with your class on character education or virtues building. If this work has been initiated in children's self-reflections rather than being externally promoted, you have one of the groundwork pieces of Restitution in place. If not, open discussion must be initiated in a non-judgmental, non-persuasive fashion. If you have a solid relationship with the person you are helping you can move right into side III. With my own children I will probably begin here on side III asking about our family beliefs and ask them if they are the kind of people they want to be, how they can solve their problems. With a guilty child I'll go to side I of the triangle to help them understand we all make mistakes and harmony can be restored. With an aggressive person I always go first to side II to seek to understand their motivation.

Asking the Restitution questions of the youth uncovers the other options they have considered and discarded. Our questions accomplish five positive ends. First, the child feels a sense of relief as she realizes she didn't do the worst thing. Second, the child is able to recognize the personal value she was protecting. Third, the child begins to have a sense of hope. Fourth, the child will exhibit absolutely no desire to lie to us. Fifth, the child will spontaneously move toward creating a solution. The final outcome of being a manager using the Restitution Triangle is greater self-understanding for the child and a strengthened relationship with us.

The Restitution Triangle

SUMMARY QUESTIONS

1. Do I believe that children are born with goodness in them?

2. Do I ask them to look inside to find the answers?

3. Do I believe they are doing the best they can to meet their needs, even at the moment of their misbehavior?

4. Am I willing to share my own foibles with those I guide and teach?

5. Have I helped my students and my own children to identify their beliefs and to think about who they want to be and how they want to treat others?

Is It Okay To Coerce?

CHAPTER TWO
OUR JOURNEY

The more profound an idea, the more obvious it appears when it is understood.
Arthur Koestler

I presented the Five Positions of Control (Punisher, Guilter, Buddy, Monitor, Manager) in my first book, *Restitution: Restructuring School Discipline.* In the last twelve years I have been on a journey with the schools. I've been working with teachers to help them understand how to be better managers. In doing this we have dealt with the following questions: What are the five positions of control? What is punishment? What is responsibility? What is monitoring? Why catch them being good? What is planning? What is a positive environment? What is the difference between a consequence and a restitution? Why is "My Job/Your Job" not enough? What is weaving between the monitor and the manager? What is the difference between monitoring and managing?

Together we have grown in our practices recognizing when we are in the punisher, guilter, or buddy mode and learning how to best use the monitor and manager. One of the things I've learned is in order to help teachers move from punishment to discipline they have to become acutely aware of their tone of voice and non-verbals. Our biggest challenge has been to realize that we can't be the manager all the time. What I've developed is a concept called "Weaving" which helps us move back and forth between creating conditions for students to be responsible for their behavior and teacher control of the class. We've all used the My Job/Your Job for the monitor, but that is not enough. We need to do the My Job/Your Job for the manager too.

This chapter will help you to be a better monitor. A better monitor is one who identifies when they are using consequences. We don't say to a student, "Your behavior is telling me you are choosing to miss recess." We are honest that we are discomforting them in the hope that they will comply. We know it is a fall back position from Restitution which is solving the problem in a creative way.

I've have also realized My Job/Your Job has led teachers back to the monitor. It is a pitfall to think that tool alone will move us to Restitution. People like the idea of having students create social contracts but find it a challenge to keep the beliefs from being applied externally. We know it is important to revisit the social contract every semester and to change it if necessary. This helps us reach our goal of students being self directed and self disciplined.

WHAT ARE THE FIVE POSITIONS OF CONTROL?

There are five ways that people attempt to control each other: punisher, guilter, buddy, monitor, and manager.

Position 1 - Punisher

The punisher uses anger, criticism, humiliation, or sarcasm. When we use this approach we are often yelling or pointing. However, punishment can also be done softly if the threat is significant. Punishment is an attempt to put the person in an inferior position.

The punisher says,

- "Do it this way or else."
- "You never get it right."
- "You're always the last one to finish."

The legacy of this position is rebellion. The person punished will not overtly confront the punisher who usually has the power, but will do something covert like graffiti on the wall or a joke at that person's expense or hurt a weaker person. If they are not afraid they will openly rebel, as does the person with a behavior disorder.

Punishers are recognized by their threats, implied or otherwise, which usually say a version of, "If you don't do what I want I'll hurt you." Youth say, "I don't care" about their work or about us because they take us out of their quality world so we can't hurt them. Once we are out of their quality world they don't try to get along with us and we have repeat offenders.

Position 2 - Guilter

Often a supervisor will overhear punishers and suggest a less aggressive approach to dealing with youth. When this happens punishers become guilters who will lower their voices and may even sound gentle as they reprimand. The person in this position uses silence, makes remarks that instill guilt, or moralizes.

The guilter says,

- "Why didn't you do what you should have done."

- "I'm disappointed in you."
- "How many times have I told you?"

Guilters play upon the youths' values to put them in a position where they feel unworthy. They use words like, "I'm very disappointed in you," and may refer to the parents saying, "What would your mother think if she knew this?" In this position authority figures are not perceived by the youth as bad, especially if much of the time they are kind. Youth then perceive the problem is that they themselves are bad. The legacy of this position is poor self esteem and what youth do is hide or deny their mistakes so as not to feel guilty. They may even lie to themselves. They say, "I'm sorry" many different ways. These youth have well learned the behavior of apologizing.

When we are in schools we do not find that teachers are anxious to punish or guilt because they know they themselves will feel badly when they do. They then move from the negative forms of control to the positive form of control—the buddy.

Position 3 - Buddy

The buddy does not hurt the youth but attempts to control the youth with praise and rewards. Many people do not recognize their agenda is to control when they persuade. Most people who use persuasion have recognized that threats and guilt hurt. However, they still believe that good behavior comes from outside influences so they apply extrinsic reinforcement to "catch them being good" and encourage repetition of the behavior. We also offer rewards to children for doing tasks they dislike doing saying, "I'll make it worth your while." The buddy position is both positive and negative. The positive part is the relationship we develop with the student. There are many disaffected students who come to school because the teacher likes them. The buddy uses friendship and humor to influence another person. The buddy says,

- "Do it for me!"
- "Remember what I did for you?"
- "I'll let you off the hook this time because it wasn't your fault."

The problem is youth will work for us but when sent to another section won't work for anyone else. Adults who manage by persuasion may say, "Do it for me." Youth who are managed by persuasion will say, "I thought you were my friend" when we try to set limits. We know we are slipping into the buddy position when we make excuses for kids or pay for their mistakes. The legacy of this position is weakness. Often children raised in affluence exhibit this trait.

Position 4 - Monitor of Rules

The monitor position is based on rules and consequences. If these are in place the monitor will need less than two minutes to redirect the youth. The monitor asks, "What's the rule? What's the consequence? What did you do? What happens to you now?" After this brief exchange the student is given a consequence. The monitor spends much time counting, tallying and charting discipline slips, sad faces, and check marks. Most teachers and youth workers have had formal training on being a monitor. This training is based on positive reinforcement, stimulus-response theory, and assertive discipline programs.

The monitor says,

- "You have earned (or lost) ten minutes of free time."
- "Do you want a sticker today?"
- "If you do that, you'll have to pay the consequences."

This approach teaches youth three things, compliance, skill at saying, "I won't do it again," and it teaches them to focus on the clock not the learning process. The legacy of the monitor position is conformity. Students in a monitoring environment ask, "What happens to me if I do this? What do I get if I do this?" These students behave to avoid discomfort or gain reward. Some parents ask, "What's wrong with conformity, isn't that enough? Why would we want to change anything if the youth are doing what we want them to do?" My question to them is, "Why would you?" There generally ensues vigorous discussion which usually encompasses two main points. If we teach them to conform as children, they transfer this conformity to the peer group in their teens. This may not be so good if the peer group has different values than your family has. Also when they leave school they may not be capable of making decisions when no one is telling them what to do. The fifth position of control, the manager, offers more. Students behave for respect of self, to be the person they want to be.

If you are finding in your school that you have more repeat offenders or that your list of rules is getting longer, it is a signal to you that the monitoring position is no longer working. Students may be "nickel and diming" you by creatively finding loopholes to your rules. This means it is time to move to belief-centered self discipline from rule-centered extrinsic discipline.

Redirecting With 30 Second Interventions

Thirty-second interventions are quick ways of redirecting a student back on task. For them to work teachers need to do a front-end load with their students. Students need to have done the My Job/Your Job activity, so when a teacher says, "What's your job?" or "What are you supposed to be doing?" they can respond. Teachers are cautioned to use the light touch in these brief encounters. A relaxed approach and calm voice are best. Also, don't hover over the student, put hands on hips, point or tap toe while waiting. Simply redirect in a friendly manner and move on as if expecting cooperation. The following are 30-second redirection phrases. They are monitoring questions and the reason they are successful is that they ask students not tell them.

> - Is what you're doing okay now?
> - What's your job now?
> - When will you be ready to start?
> - What can I do to help you so you can …?
> - What's the rule? Can you do that?
> - What are you supposed to be doing?
> - It looks like you have a problem? How can I help you solve it?
> - Do you want to figure out a better way? How can I help?
> - Is what you're doing now helping or hurting our lesson?

Remember these words are only 10% of the message you are sending, 35% is your tone and 55% are your non-verbals.

Position 5 - Manager of Restitution

This person knows how to do everything the monitor does and will use that approach as a fall-back position. However, the helper who prefers to focus on restitution first is teaching youth to be self-managers. The recipient of this approach is asked to work to invent a solution. The emphasis is not on designing a consequence. This person works *with* the student to figure out how to repair the mistake.

The manager says,

- "How are you going to make things right?"
- "What's your plan to solve the problem?"
- "What kind of person do you want to be?"
- "What's your plan to fix it? When can you have it done? How will it get you stronger and help the group?"

Rather than removing youth from the group, managers help them return to the group. Restitution also holds the potential for the youth to become stronger. Every time one fixes a problem and ties it to the person one wants to be, there is less chance the person will reoffend. They have not just conformed to show us the behavior we want to see, they are becoming more of the person they want to be in their quality world. The questions of the manager are, "What do we believe? Do you believe it? If you believe it do you want to fix it? If you fix it, what does it say about you?"

The first four positions are ones where the teacher does something *to* the student and is taking the responsibility for the student's behavior. The last position, the manager, is one where the teacher is doing something *with* the student—letting the student take responsibility for his or her own behavior.

Our Journey

And as managers, we help students examine their actions and make internal evaluations of what they can do to repair their mistakes. This is restitution.

Restitution is founded on the following principles:

➢ We respect each individual's view of the world. (Control Theory)

➢ We create conditions of safety and space for reflection so the brain can take in and evaluate information and create moral meaning. (Brain-Based Learning)

➢ We reduce both rewards and punishments, which deflect youth from developing self-discipline. (Alfie Kohn)

➢ We develop internal moral sense rather than forcing conformity. (Aboriginal Beliefs)

➢ We uphold bottom lines consistently and publicly so people feel safe. (Violence Research)

How were you raised? Also ask yourself how the people around you are behaving. Are they rebelling or saying "I'm sorry" a lot? Are they dependent and compliant? Do they have a strong sense of self? If you look at how they are acting with you, you can then read the chart below to find out what you are doing. Remember the first four positions are external discipline. The fifth teaches students autonomy and so they choose to be responsible to others. Edward Deci in *Why We Do What We Do* says, "It is important to us to remember people's interest in changing begins with their taking genuine interest in their own motivations."[6] Only when one makes an idea personal can it be a base of new creativity.

---

[6] Edward Deci and Richard Flaste. *Why We Do What We Do.* New York: Penguin Books, 1996.

Five Positions of Control

	Avoid Pain		Reward from Others		Respecting Self
	PUNISHER	**GUILTER**	**BUDDY**	**MONITOR**	**MANAGER**
Teacher Does	Yells and Points	Preaches and "Shoulds"	Makes excuses for them	Counts and Measures	Asks questions
Teacher Says	If you don't do it I'll...	You should have known better	Do it for me	What's the rule?	What do we believe?
Legacy	Rebel Blame	Hide Deny Lie	Dependency	Conformity	Strengthen
Student Says	I don't care	I'm sorry	I thought you were my friend	How high, how far?	What can I do to fix it?
Student Outcome	Repeat offense	Low self-esteem	Weakness	Consequence oriented	Self restitution

EXTRINSIC MOTIVATION — INTRINSIC MOTIVATION

WHAT IS PUNISHMENT: ARE YOU A PUNISHER?

Punishment can be either hurting or guilting. Hurting can be physical or verbal. People who see punishment as the answer say that what we need is a bigger hammer. If we had that, the kids would be good. Conventional teachers are not flexible. They say things like "My way or the highway." They truly believe there is one right way for learning to take place, their way. Questions from students are seen as an affront to their authority rather than as opportunities to dialogue. Challenges to the curriculum are frowned upon. When there is jockeying for position the teacher searches for a more severe or unexpected consequence with which to surprise the student. Sometimes conventional teachers set students up or they may even aggravate them to blow up when a special event is in the offing. When this happens as a consequence the student is denied the opportunity to attend. The teacher may smugly say, "You should have thought about this before." It is punitive.

This approach to management erodes relationships and nurtures in the students a desire to get even or to leave our school. Are conventional teachers bad people? Not usually. Their difficulty arises from the fact that they are focused on their product – the grades and homework rather than on the process of learning and they use this yardstick to measure their success. What we perceive as their resistance is really a pro-product stance rather than an understanding of the process of collaborative learning.

If you have a colleague who believes in punishment, patience is needed. These persons are where they are at this time because it is somewhat comfortable for them. Conventional discipline gives a sense of being in control and that feeling is important to all of us. Often conventional teachers have attempted in the past to be more democratic and the class has taken advantage of them. What these teachers can be invited to consider is the concept that educating students and sharing the power can result in an even greater sense of control once the process is complete. The first step for a conventional teacher to take is to study the difference between punishment and consequences and then to be sure the consequences they apply are fair, reasonable and expected. The second step for this teacher is to quietly redirect the students rather than threatening them. The third step is to begin to improve relationships by using the tools of weaving and restitution. You will learn these in the next chapters.

Do you have staff members who believe we need to punish students more? When someone in a school says, "My dad gave me the belt and I'm a better person for it." I ask, "Did you know that even if you were hit your parent loved you?" They say, "Yes." Then I ask, "Did you learn some skills from your parent that have helped you in life?" They will say, "Yes." Then I say, "Even if you were punished you had a success identity strong enough to absorb it." The people who were not loved or not taught by their parents never say, "I'm a better person for being hit." These people are in a failure identity. When faced with punishment they go into rebellion or withdrawal. However punishment only appears to work with people who have a success identity. What really happens is that they absorb the negative experience. They are not strengthened by receiving punishment. It is an illusion that it works. This is not to say that hitting is ever acceptable or that if you have a good relationship it is okay to do it. I don't mean to minimize the damage. I tell this story only to counteract the illusion that it was the punishment that was the change agent. It was not.

I think of my own children. I know there were times they were punished. However, they forgave me because of the strength of the relationship.
Punishment does not work for a person who already feels like a failure. I learned this when I was a trainer of correction workers in the Saskatoon prison system. There were many staff who believed in punishment. I asked those who believed in punishment, "Could you as a child have figured out a way to behave better without being hit or punished verbally?" They always answered, "Yes." I believe we can get change without hurting and this change will be permanent. If a child thinks things through and then does something, it is because they believe it's the right thing to do not because they fear being punished.

Our penal system is punishment and the majority of prison inmates have a history of school failure. Punishment increases a negative attitude rather than a positive one. It increases pain rather than alleviating it and it destroys the potential for involvement. As a matter of fact, one criterion to apply to an incident in order to evaluate whether it is punishment is to assess if it decreases involvement. If the relationships are weakened, punishment has been used. Because punishment is something which is imposed, the responsibility for punishment is assumed by the punisher. The people punished are not a partner to this consequence. Nothing is done by them. Something is done to them. They feel powerless. As a response they either give up or try to get revenge. I was the director of training for five prisons from 1980 to 1981. I declined a promotion when I realized the majority of inmates had dropped out of school. I decided to return to education and to do the best I could to help teachers and parents see that punishment doesn't work.

RESPONSIBILITY: WHAT DOES IT REALLY MEAN?

In many of the districts with which I have worked the word Responsible has been used in implementing the Restitution program. For example one of the programs on the west coast was called Responsible Decision Making. One in the Midwest was called Responsibility Training and a third one in Canada tied Restitution to the provincial guideline of Social Responsibility. The word responsible was chosen partly to avoid using the word restitution which in many people's minds has a correctional system connotation. The other reason is that all parents want their children to be responsible. However as I reflect I believe that the word responsibility can inadvertently lead us away from internal character growth into compliance. Let's look at the definition of responsibility. Some of the definitions of responsible are obliged or expected to account for; accountable, answerable, deserving credit or blame, trustworthy or reliable, involving obligation or duties, able to tell right from wrong; able to think and act reasonably.

If the most common meaning of the word responsible, is obliged or accountable, no wonder we have ended up with an emphasis on compliance. Accountable for what? Obliged to whom? The word responsible leads us into a model which is certain to have echoes of a stimulus response orientation. When parents or teachers or public officials talk about responsibility they most often mean youth are obliged to follow our expectations and respond to our rules. Thus we gain compliance. While this is necessary in a society it is a monitoring model not a self discipline model. The majority of people will be responsible only when supervised. They will be accountable when we have sanctions to apply to those we find irresponsible. When we lift these penalties they go back to doing what they want to do.

WHAT IS MONITORING?

Monitoring is supervising. When we supervise we take responsibility for the behavior of those we oversee. In using consequences one learns to separate one's personal relationships with the students from one's role as a disciplinarian. We develop a definition of our responsibility as one who is the enforcer of the rules. We use terms like "I'm in a position where I have to...invoke this consequence." As a monitor we may even do a My Job/Your Job to tell students that as a person we might not care about incomplete work or uncleaned lunch trays, but our job requires us to enforce the rules that others have made. This is pretty clever as it makes the administrator or the board to be the "bad guy" and us to be the "good guy" just following directions and from time to time shrugging sympathetically.

When I worked at the Educator Training Center, I learned that it was important for me and the students to make up the rules together. I saw this as a real evolution toward democracy. I engaged my class in vigorous discussion. I failed to recognize that I, myself as a member of society, would not be much interested in having input to measures devised to assure my conformity nor would I find it attractive to develop a slate of consequences to which I might be subject in the future. However, I noticed when I worked the rule making process with my students, that they were quite enthusiastic and sometimes even suggested sanctions which I as the teacher had to reject as too severe. It appeared to me that during the process they seldom conceived of themselves as rule breakers and even took some perverse pleasure in setting out a sliding scale of consequences that they envisioned off-task fellow classmates would merit.

Once we had our rules set out and the consequences enumerated we hung them on the wall. When a student misbehaved we could gesture toward our rule list, have them read it or read it for them. We then asked, "If this is the rule and you broke it, what happens now?" If the student lowered his or her head or looked at us defiantly we took some satisfaction in restating the consequence. I have even been known to say somewhat piously, "I didn't make this up. We all decided what would happen." I also used phrases like, "Your behavior is telling me you're choosing to have this consequence." The problem was it created conditions that weren't good for learning or cooperating. However, as teachers, we used consequences with some satisfaction, holding it over the students' heads.

BE A BUDDY AND CATCH THEM BEING GOOD

Somewhere along the line I learned the phrase "catch them being good" and began to see that if I gave them positive reinforcement for on-task behavior I wouldn't have to invoke so many consequences. I began a vigorous personal campaign of social rewards and compliments directed toward students when they were conforming. I also started giving rewards for compliance. For awhile I felt better. Students liked the rewards and they even began approaching me to evaluate their on-task behavior in order to get some more positive strokes. For awhile "paying them to be good" seemed to be working.

Despite the apparent benefits of this method I grew a little worried when I found students cheating to get a reward. Students were sometimes also seen buying stickers at the store and putting them on their books so they could look successful. I became more concerned when I saw incidents of the group bullying one class member to get him to conform to the group so the group would get their privilege. I heard one situation where primary students were licking the stamps on their wrists and trying to transfer them to another's. One time a student was beat up and his stickers stolen. Still this process was the best I knew at the time.

Parents began to object that problem students sometimes had extra privileges. We tried to educate them about individual differences. I said things like, "Equal isn't always the same" but the questions remained. I began to not like my job so well. Students began to notice that those who misbehaved were getting more rewards than students who were on task, as they had more plans and each plan had built into it a positive reinforcement.

As time went on I began to make some other observations. I noticed I had to vary the rewards and use them intermittently to keep up the students' interest. I began asking students to set rewards that they would be willing to work for. I started to realize that I was spending a lot of money on prizes and treats and I was getting tired of giving positive verbal reinforcement.

WHAT IS A POSITIVE ENVIRONMENT?

The key to a positive environment is in how we are perceiving the students. As Dr. Glasser would ask, "Have you put the student into your Quality World? Has the student put school, school work and their teacher into their Quality World." Dr. Anderson, principal of Sheridan Hills Elementary School, says when she approaches students who have problems they come towards her not turn away from her because she has taken the time to know them, understand them and love them.

To create a needs satisfying environment my colleagues and I began to have class meetings[7] each morning. We developed provocative topics which helped develop involvement and perspective taking and we had students develop topics and lead meetings. Some schools I have worked with used developmentally appropriate practices. A positive class environment was built by teachers being aware of age appropriate characteristics, learning

---

[7] Diane Gossen, Ed. *Class Meetings*. Saskatoon: Chelsom Consultants Limited, 1988.

Our Journey

styles, arrangement of the classroom, constructivist approach, multiage and looping, and a literacy rich environment. All of these made the classroom a more inviting place for students.

Staff evolved in their teaching practices until at one point they began to question if we were taking too much responsibility for the students' happiness. We were spending much of our time redesigning to create an environment where the student's needs would be met. We saw this as our job and some of us even felt we had failed if we hadn't sufficiently modified the class environment so as to accommodate the needs of all our students.

The next step in my evolution was to brainstorm with my colleagues to help the student find a better behavior he or she could use to meet the presenting need. I stayed in this mode for about ten years, each year becoming more skilled at creating alternatives for kids to meet their needs. We made lots of plans.

WHAT IS PLANNING?

For most of us our training has focused on planning. There are many of you reading this that have held domain over whole file cabinets of plans. The plans I recall had many common elements. Usually there was first a detailed description of the problem which took quite a bit of time to establish. Then there was an assumption of blame or an admission of error with the child writing, "I'll tell them I'm sorry." This was followed by a plan to do better next time. The majority of the plans I have reviewed said something like, "I know I was wrong and I won't do it again." We felt relieved. These plans gave us the illusion things would be getting better and they did – for awhile. However, sooner or later the child found it too difficult to comply and they slipped back to their old ways or they invented a new behavior that met their needs, but may well have disrupted ours.

It has been interesting to me to see the many evaluations of plans as we attempted to revise them so they would be effective. I think most of us felt the answer was in the plan and it was only a matter of getting a good one. I can also remember waiting for the child to give the plan I already had in my mind. I was leaning forward and nodding and I used a lot of rhetorical questions. "You know what I mean don't you. This would be better for you wouldn't it? Your teacher would be happy if you did this, right?"

When the plans were not kept we asked students, "Why didn't you do it?" They, thinking we searched to assign blame, answered "I don't know" or made excuses or even lied. We then fell back on our consequences and frequently made more elaborate and more specific plans that boxed in students until they felt they had only two choices – to conform or to rebel. A few dropped out of the game altogether.

The word plan, a perfectly good word, began to be synonymous with consequences. Students half-heartedly or abruptly said, "Just give me a plan form. I'll do it." There were many times when I felt I worked harder than the students. I cared more about the plan than they did. When I became disheartened, I began to compile all their unsuccessful plans to bolster my own position when talking with administration or the parents. It was clear, I thought, that I had certainly done my job. One student actually had 123 plans which we had helped her make. She looked somewhat triumphant as we presented the stack to her parents. Her smile seemed to say, "I've defeated another teacher." We were tired, tired of planning, tired of caring more about the plan than did the student, tired of trying to make her do what we wanted. However, we also had significant successes where students really turned around their behavior. We congratulated ourselves and did workshops to teach others what we knew. At one point I realized I was taking responsibility for creating a need-satisfying environment rather than teaching the youth to be independent, to manage themselves in a world which is not always need-fulfilling. I also noticed that on some occasions the success of the plan itself seemed to be its own reward for the student. I became very interested in this second group of students who wanted change for its own sake.

WHAT IS THE DIFFERENCE BETWEEN A CONSEQUENCE AND A RESTITUTION?

In this section we are going to first look at the difference between a consequence and Restitution. Reasonably agreed upon consequences of irresponsible behaviors are not punishment. Logical consequences express the reality of a social order. In any given situation it is essential that the rules be learned, in order for adequate functioning to ensue. The setting up of consequences and the understanding of rules eliminates the element of the unexpected. This is because consequences are the same as punishment except that they are "lite" punishment. Consequences discomfort while punishment hurts. When youth are not self disciplined we may have to use consequences until they learn to manage their own behavior and to solve their problems. This is not bad. However we must remember consequences are not Restitution. They are monitoring tool and are a fall back position from restitution questions which are restorative.

I was invited to work with a district in Iowa a year after they started Restitution. One hundred staff from several schools had prepared for me a list of restitutions they were using. It was an eye opener to all of us to see where Restitution was going off the track. In the following chart the restitutions that were really consequences are marked with a "C".

Restitution for Frequent Misbehaviors

The three problems that we believe needed restitution are:

1. Students talking when the teacher is teaching.
2. Not standing in line.
3. Hands and feet on others.

Plans for restitution:

1. The student chooses to miss recess to think. *C*
2. The student chooses to miss free time. *C*
3. The student chooses to miss snack time. *C*
4. The student will stay after school. *C*
5. If a student marks on another's paper, the student who has the problem will make another paper for their friend.
6. A student will make a poster at home and share it at school.
7. The student will fix the problem in some way.
8. A student can replace an object that is destroyed using their own effort.

Half of their restitutions penalized rather than strengthened. They were really consequences though they were called Restitution. Though they had pay forward potential the focus was more on discomforting. This explained what they had told me which was that Restitution worked only sometimes. My guess was it worked when it was not a consequence.

WHY IS MY JOB/ YOUR JOB NOT ENOUGH?

What people like and use most from *Restitution: Restructuring School Discipline* is the "My Job/Your Job" activity. This is a four part T-Chart that is used to outline how two jobs differ. This chart is used to clarify responsibilities of both parties as well as the authority that each person is given to do their job. Examples are teacher/student, principal/ assistant principal, counselor/ social worker, special education teacher/ teaching assistant, and parents/school. Wherever there is a grey area, clarification is needed so each party can feel confident and in control of their tasks. The 'my job is not' and 'your job is not' parts of the chart are especially important to do and they can include some humor.

Almost every Restitution university assignment I have read extols this T-Chart of responsibilities along with the thirty second phrases to redirect students back to what they agreed to do. I stand by this process. It has always worked well for me because it helps people to create common pictures of who should be doing what and it can be used at all levels of the organization. However it is important to state that My Job/Your Job falls in the monitoring category because it has to do with the division of power. It is not the same as doing a Social Contract which has to do with our common values and personal ideals.

The reason I think My Job/Your Job is so popular is that a decade ago when we first taught Restitution workshops it filled an important role. It assisted teachers in making a transition from criticizing students to redirecting them. They found they could stop being angry. They could even give up guilt. These behaviors weren't necessary to gain student compliance. All that was necessary was to create expectations together then refer students back to what we had decided and then ask them to do what they agreed to do. It saved teachers a lot of energy and preserved relationships. However, what My Job/Your Job did not do was tap creativity and individuality. Students became tired of hearing. "What's your job?" much as they had become tired of hearing "What's the rule?" And teachers got tired of asking. One teacher said to me, "I've asked, 'What's your job?' thirty times today and I'm exhausted." One kid even said to me, "I know now you're going to ask me how you can help me get started." Here are examples below:

Bus Driver and Student

My Job Is To	Your Job Is To
• Transport kids	• Respect every one on the bus
• Safety on bus	• Stay seated
• Safe boarding and discharge	• Keep hands to self
• Be on time	• Normal voice
• Respect every one on the bus	• Be on time
• Clean bus & fuel bus	• Cooperate
My Job Is Not	**Your Job Is Not**
• Pick up after your belongings	• To do my job
• To take or give abuse	• Discipline others
• Wait for you if you have detention	• To take or give abuse

Primary School Teacher & Students

Teacher My Job Is...	Students Your Job Is...
• Be prepared	• Be prepared
• Be on time	• Listen
• Plan	• Follow rules
• Teach	• Be positive
• Build self esteem	• Complete tasks on time
• Meet the needs of student	• Cooperate with all
• Keep up with new information	

My Job Is Not...	Your Job Is Not...
• To baby-sit	• To do my job
• To referee	• To discipline others or to tell others what to do
• To become frustrated with curriculum	• To tattle
• To solve problems for them	• To do someone else's work
• To put in mandatory overtime	
• To do janitorial things	
• To decide a dress code	
• To listen to tattling	

Intermediate Teacher & Student

Teacher My Job Is...	Student Your Job Is...
• To teach	• To learn
• Evaluate/grade	• To try
• Coordinate learning environment	• To do best
• To continue learning	• Be prepared
• To communicate with parents	• Be positive
• To be prepared	• Respect others
• To enforce rules	• Clean up after self
• To keep records	• To listen
	• To evaluate own work

My Job Is Not...	Your Job Is Not...
• To take or give abuse	• To take or give abuse
• To be a social coordinator	• To complain
• To be an emperor, dictator	• To destroy property
• To clean up after students	• To do my job, or other's jobs
• To provide food, supplies	• To evaluate others

Bumping it up

What we need to do is take the components of the My Job/Your Job and bump up these job descriptions by asking, "Why do we have these expectations?" This moves us into Restitution by tapping the beliefs in order to move on to the manager. The "why" can be either answered by finding the need or by identifying a belief. Now we are working with the moral part of the student's brain. Then we ask the person to create a new way to meet the need or to honor the belief instead of merely saying, "I'll do what I'm told." If the student is continually not meeting an expectation we can be sure his or her needs are not being met by complying with the rule. That is the reason we have non compliance. If we request a person to comply with a plan that doesn't meet their need we can gain initial agreement. However it will last only a few days, and will not give us the long term solution that restitution plan can create. We need to go beyond redirecting them and thanking them for their compliance. For a long term solution Restitution plans should satisfy both the offender and the person hurt.

What are the personal jobs of the manager and the learner?

What we need to do is move to a second stage with restitution and create a My Job/Your Job chart which delineates the manager's job. This job is to elicit beliefs, create a climate for students to do moral reflection and to create solutions. The student's job will be to think for themselves to learn to self-manage and to self-restitute.

Here is an example of a "My Job/Your Job" for the **Manager**.

My Personal Job as a Teacher	My Personal Job as a Student
Teacher I Want To Be • Is a life long learner. • Seeks to understand others. • Ask lots of questions • Seeks many perspectives when teaching and discussing. • Asks "How can I best teach you?" • Says and believes, "It's o.k. to make a mistake, its how we learn." • Creates conditions for people to dialogue about our beliefs and to participate in a social contract. • Models self restitution and the restitution triangle questions. • Talks about and teaches basic needs. • Collapses conflict. • Has fun learning. • Knows about how the brain works.	**Student I Want To Be** • Learns new things. • Questions everything. • Thinks for self. • Learns self restitution. • Identifies my own needs and recognizes others needs. • Uses collapse conflict for win-win • Invents new solutions. • Learns about behavior parts. • Has fun; it's how we learn. • Follows through. • Learns how my brain works. • Is a team member. • Learns and uses the restitution. • Takes safe risks. • Thinks about the ideal person to be. • Thinks about family beliefs. • Helps make a class social contract with others
Teacher I Don't Want To Be • Telling you what to think. • Criticizing or shaming you. • Thinking for you. • Doing your work. • Punishing you.	**Student I Don't Want To Be** • Telling you what you want to hear. • Saying "sorry" to get off the hook. • Watching the clock. • Telling others they are wrong.

WHAT IS WEAVING BETWEEN
THE MONITOR AND THE MANAGER?

When we try to be a manager to help the youth self-manage sometimes they close us out. They don't want to change or look at their actions. They want to keep doing what they are doing. However, what they are doing has consequences for others. These consequences are not positive. When this happens we need to weave back and be in the monitor position. The monitor gives a warning and metes out consequences. A monitor uses external control and a warning. A monitor is not a punisher but is calm and firm. A monitor says if you don't…I have to… (consequence). We all know how to do this and we need to do this when we find we are working harder than the person we're trying to help. If we practise this we are saving our energy for the students who want to learn.

When we have given the warning (monitor) it is crucial to weave back to the manager and say I would rather be helping you … (fix it). If the child continues to be rude after we say the manager part, weave back to the monitor and apply the consequence. By practising "weaving" you will find many times the youth will fix their problem and gain strength. At home it would sound like this, "If you don't clean up your mess we won't be having the party on Saturday. This is not the conversation I want to be having with you. I would rather talk about what we're going to do when we have the party on Saturday." The challenge for us is to conceive of and verbalize the positive interchange we want to be having. I taught many teachers in training early in my career. I blush now to think of how I modeled giving the warning (monitor) and then assuming a toe to toe position expecting compliance.

Weaving Between

MONITOR   MANAGER

If you don't _____ I have to _____.	I would rather _____
(Give you a consequence–discomfort.)	(Fix it. We both get what we need.)

You may weave more than once. "If you don't write the test I can't give you a grade. That's not what I want. I want you to have credit for this class." If the student says, "I don't care, give me a zero," we have to weave back to the monitor saying, "I can't give you marks for what you don't do." Say what the mark will be. Then finish always on the manager who says "But it is not what I want." Here are a few examples of weaving. Notice how the manager always finds a way to get both needs met.

"If you don't come to the practice, you'll be sitting on the bench at the next game (monitor). But I'd rather be talking to you about what's your plan to get here or to find someone to help you practise the skills you miss at practice so you can be ready to play with the team at the next game. What do you want?" (manager)

"If you don't clean up the lunch table, you will have to stay in for recess (monitor). I would rather have you go outside and have fun with your friends. That's what I want. What about you?" (manager)

"If you don't share the equipment, I'll have you work alone (monitor). But that's not what I want to do. I'd rather help you figure out how to be a cooperative member of this group. What do you want?" (manager)

A principal can weave with their staff by saying, "If these reports aren't done we'll be sitting here Friday at 3:30pm. (Monitor)   That's not where I want to be. I want to be on the golf course. What about you folks? Can we work it out?" (Manager)

As much as possible when the consequence is stated it should be a natural consequence rather than something we create to personally discomfort the student. For example:

No work	therefore	No grade
Hurt others	therefore	Be alone
Don't learn the skills	therefore	Sit on the bench

We want to do the monitor from the position that it is our job to: check on work, keep the playground safe, teach sports skills, and give grades. Remember the weaving tool is the second line of action. The first tool is to use the 30-second interventions to redirect. This is because the first part of weaving statement puts us "toe to toe" in adversity with the student. By far the most important part of the weaving statement is the positive intent of the manager to solve things together based on our beliefs.

We want to weave from being "toe to toe" which is the monitor to being "shoulder to shoulder" where we are on the same side as the student looking at the task together, helping each other. However, if students spin out on us after hearing the monitor they never do get our manager words. This is why a calm tone and body posture is so important.

A special education teacher said to me, "Why do we have to do the monitor anyway? Can't we just do the manager?" When you practise weaving the monitor will gradually atrophy and then you'll be left with the manager or redirecting. However at the beginning it is important to put in the monitor. This is because students are so used to being monitored that if they think you don't know the consequences they will push to find the limits. They will think nothing happens here, that they just talk to you. It is a transition for students to move from being monitored to self-management. We need to work with them gradually.

One teacher said she had a difficult student and had been thinking she couldn't take her on the field trip. She was going to say, "I want you to go on the field trip but if you can't stay with the group I can't take you." Evaluate this statement. Can you see a flaw? The statement is great but it has the manager first. By ending on the monitor it sets up adversity.

It is better to say, "If you can't stay with the group and be safe I can't take you on the field trip. That is not what I want. I would rather have you with the group because we're going to have a lot of fun and the rides are free. What do you want?"

When you practise the weave, keep in mind that when you are doing the monitor you are using consequences. When you are doing the manager you are drawing an ideal picture of the outcome you desire. You can't make the person choose this but we can offer the possibility. This is not a bribe; it is how we want to be with them in the future.

The charts below also illustrate the difference between the monitor and the manager. The monitor focuses on rules and consequences. The manager focuses on beliefs and fixing the problem.

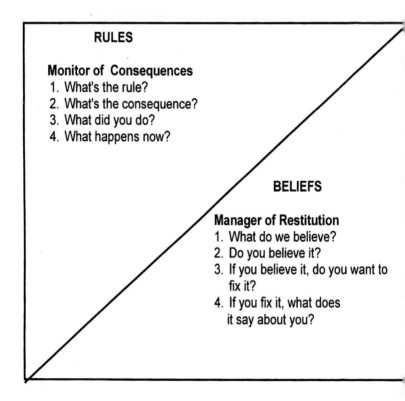

RULES

Monitor of Consequences
1. What's the rule?
2. What's the consequence?
3. What did you do?
4. What happens now?

BELIEFS

Manager of Restitution
1. What do we believe?
2. Do you believe it?
3. If you believe it, do you want to fix it?
4. If you fix it, what does it say about you?

Story: What Do We Believe About Safety In the Pool?

The story below shows how to move from the monitor to the manager, how to move from rules and consequences to beliefs and fixing problems, and how to move from compliance to self discipline.

One Sunday I had driven one hundred miles to spend the day with my four grandchildren. We were in the backyard when Mitch the eight year old pulled his six year old brother into the deep end of the pool. His dad said "Mitch get out of the pool and sit on a chair for ten minutes." This was interesting. I could see they had rules and Mitch was having the privilege of the pool removed because he had broken a rule. Then my son in law said "Now you watch him Diane." I thought, I don't want to be a policeman to my grandson all afternoon! I thought about using Restitution but since they hadn't yet done their family beliefs, I didn't know how to approach it. As I thought about it, it was clear to me that Mitch knew the rules. I asked him what they were. He said no going in the pool without an adult, no jumping backwards and no fighting. When he said no fighting I had to resist the urge in myself to jump in and ask "Well what were you doing?" However I knew that would be going for fault and Restitution has to seek the belief. So I asked, "Why do you have those rules Mitch?" He said, "So no one gets hurt." I asked, Do you believe it's important to be safe?" He said, "Yes" and I knew I had the belief I needed. I then said to Mitch "My job is to watch you when you go back in the pool so if I see something that is not safe I'm going to call out and ask you what do we believe about safety in the pool, and you'll see if you can fix the situation to be safe." Mitch agreed and since ten minutes was up he went back in the pool.

We had a beautiful afternoon. I only had to call out once. When I said "Mitch what do we believe about safety?" He turned around, gave me a big smile and said "I can fix it Grandma," and he did. Now this may seem like a simple story, but just think of how different it could have been if we had stayed on the rules. When I saw the second mistake I'd have called out "Mitch!" No answer, "Young man I'm talking to you!" What look do you think I'd have seen on his face? Maybe fear, maybe annoyance, and I'd have been saying, "Mitch, this time it will be twenty minutes. If it happens again you're out of the whole afternoon." We'd have had three hours of adversity instead of three hours of cooperation.

SUMMARY – MONITOR-MANAGER ASSESSMENT

Below is a chart to help you assess whether you are in monitor or manager position. The next chapter will focus on the manager.

MONITOR	**MANAGER**
◻ Defining my job/your job ◻ Redirecting with 30 second interventions ◻ Rules ◻ Consequences ◻ Bottom Line ◻ Offense one, two, three ◻ Warnings ◻ Time out in class area ◻ Time out in another class ◻ Time out in planning room ◻ Isolation area ◻ Suspension ◻ Expulsion	◻ Involvement - talking with student about something of mutual interest that is not the problem ◻ Teaching the basic needs ◻ Teaching the components of behavior and how the brain works ◻ Teaching cognitive reframing ◻ Using a healing circle with a talking piece ◻ Doing social contract on class beliefs ◻ Teaching conflict resolution and the peace table ◻ Teaching the restitution questions
Increase supervision/consequence	Educate and Redesign

CHAPTER THREE

SHOULDER TO SHOULDER

Management means, in the last analysis, the substitution of thought for brawn and muscle, of knowledge for folklore and superstition, and of cooperation for force...
Peter Drucker

Do you know the difference between toe to toe and shoulder to shoulder? Have you ever found yourself standing toe to toe with a child? How about your spouse? How about a colleague? How do you feel when this is happening? Is it a good feeling? Is your stomach tense or calm? Are you flushed? Do you feel like fighting? Is this productive? What needs to happen next? If you stand toe to toe will it get better or worse? Do you think you want to change it? If so, why not try shoulder to shoulder?

The moment you stand shoulder to shoulder with someone you are both looking in the same direction. If you are looking in the same direction you could be looking at the same thing. If you are looking at goals you have created together it is a good thing, and you can help each other. If you help each other you are no longer toe to toe. Take a deep breath. Your shoulders go down your stomach relaxes. Ask yourself, "If I do what I did last time will it get me what I want next time? Is what I am doing getting me what I want? What is it we both want for our relationship, for the task we have to do together? Do we want to be shoulder to shoulder to accomplish it?" If so why not assume that position, move shoulder to shoulder, sit side by side and ask, "How can we both get what we need?" Talk about what you need. Ask what he or she needs.

Restitution is a shoulder to shoulder process. Restitution restores harmony between individuals and within the group. I was once asked to view a tape of a restorative circle for two nine year old girls who had shop lifted. I didn't have to see more than a minute of the tape to know it was not restorative. The two little girls were in the center of the circle. People were pointing at them. They were hanging on to each other and sobbing. There was no adult or peer shoulder to shoulder with them. I was asked to comment and said "This was not a healing circle. It was a shaming circle." When questioned further I told them that in my experience in the north with aboriginal circles everyone sat together a the same level and an elder usually sat with the offenders and often spoke for them so they felt supported. More than once I heard the phrase, "They know what they did has hurt someone and they want to learn a better way." This story can remind us to always sit with the youth shoulder to shoulder to lend them our strength and to look for common ground. What do we both want to be better?

The rest of this chapter will further define Restitution. The following guidelines will distinguish Restitution healing practices from other discipline programs.

- ➤ Restitution is not a payback; it is a pay forward.
- ➤ Restitution restores relationships.
- ➤ Restitution is an invitation not coercion.
- ➤ Restitution teaches the person to look inside.
- ➤ Restitution is looking for the basic need behind the problem.
- ➤ Self restitution is the most powerful tool.
- ➤ Restitution is about "being" not "doing".
- ➤ Restitution strengthens.
- ➤ Restitution focuses on solutions.
- ➤ Restitution restores one to the group.

RESTITUTION IS NOT A PAYBACK;
IT IS A PAY FORWARD

Restitution need not be money or a clean up or an apology. In the correctional system restitution has come to mean, "Pay the fine or do the time." It is not restorative. This makes the restitution only a payback with a specified consequence if the payback is not made. This results in the person focusing on the act of restitution rather than the internal healing process. In North Dakota it was very difficult for us to begin a program called Restitution because each week the paper published a list of offenders required by the courts to pay restitution. Parents were initially reluctant to support a program they mistakenly saw associated with crime. The second problem is that the payback brings the illusion that the slate is wiped clean as if the offense had never happened. It discourages an examination of the underlying structure of the problem to identify how to resolve conflict. While Restitution may include a payback, it is a secondary part of the process of healing and initiated from inside the offender. Real healing occurs through this person desiring to make an amend. The focus is not just on reparation to the victim but on being a better person and paying forward to others the goodness invested in us.

What Is A Pay Forward?

A pay forward is something wherein a person learns about a better way to be. They gain an understanding they can use over and over again to be a better person. Mandela and Bishop Tutu's Truth and Reconciliation Commission is such an example. The young men who have murdered people, if they admit it and answer the questions of family members of the dead, are taken back in by the village to be nurtured and taught.

Several years ago the program 60 Minutes Live featured a family whose daughter had been killed by a gang of youths in Soweto just before the disbanding of apartheid. They said they were grieving terribly until their prayers showed them a restorative route to take. They decided to take three months each year to go to Soweto. They built a bakery, a carpentry shop and a school for the youth of the community. The eleven year old sister of one of the boys who had killed their daughter became a student in the school. They said now when the wheels of their plane hit the tarmac they feel that their daughter is with them and they are at peace. This story is an example of a pay forward created for healing. Another example is from the movie *Pay Forward*. Trevor, a grade seven student, decides he can change the world by doing an unexpected big favor for a person in need. All he asks of this person is that he or she do a good deed for three others. This pay forward is different from a pay back and has potential to make a better world.

What is a Payback?

A payback is something a person does to repair a harm. It is a reparation, an action or a concrete repayment. It probably should be named a pay out. It is usually done to avoid pain or to get back in good standing. It is finite. The person who makes it considers they have righted their wrong and are finished with the situation. To make a payback is not wrong, but it is not usually strengthening. Rather it is a relief to have it over with.

What is a Negative Payback?

"You're gonna get yours!" This is a negative payback. It is a vengeful action to even a score. It is done by people who have been punished so they feel they have to get even. This kind of payback has a long life because it keeps the conflict alive. An example of this is a story I was told to explain to me the conflict between Croats and Serbs when I was teaching in Croatia during the war. It is an old folk tale. A farmer rescues a genie who has been trapped in a bottle. He is offered one wish by the genie in return for the liberation. The condition attached by the genie is that his Serbian neighbor will get twice as much. With little thought the Croatian replies, "Tear out one of my eyes." This tale is an example of deep seated generational conflict. This is revenge as a payback for old hurts.

I have had the disheartening experience of seeing a pay forward shift into a payback. When this occurs it is often after a heartfelt restitution has been created. One of the adults feels the need to add on an unexpected consequence to discomfort the child. Another way this can happen is if we decide to remonstrate or guilt the child, just for good measure at the end. This can shift the youth from making the amend because she feels it is the right thing to do, to following through to avoid the pain of guilt. This is a sad thing to see. One of the reasons a restorative process has a circle keeper is to prevent this from happening. The one who has done wrong is so vulnerable when they are in the pay forward position, that if they are shamed the emotional door slams shut and they are less likely to trust again.

A Pay Forward Not a Pay Back

The principal of one of our schools sent this Restitution story. It is one I want to use to illustrate the difference between restitution as a pay back and restitution as a pay forward. An elementary student is sent to the office from the playground because he has urinated on another's pants.

I Didn't Mean It - Payback

Several weeks ago, a grade four student, Joey, came hobbling into the office stiff-legged during lunch recess. With arms stretched outward and a disgruntled look, he exclaimed, "Somebody went to the washroom on my pant leg!" "What?" gasped the school secretary. "What?" I echoed in disbelief. My immediate reaction was, "I've already made up my mind...this is a no-brainer. Whoever did this is out of here. They're suspended out of this school."

I had Joey try to sit. He preferred to stand...I really didn't blame him. In walked Ziggy sobbing and shaking uncontrollably. I knew I was about the hear the story. I'm so glad I had kept my immediate thoughts to myself.

Ziggy joined me alone in my office and began, "Well, at lunch today, one of the parents brought in McDonald's for lunch and offered me a super-sized drink. After I finished it, of course I went out for recess and it was very cold. All of a sudden I had to go to the washroom and there was no teacher on duty in sight. I couldn't wait. I went over to the trashcan at the far end of the playground and four of my friends surrounded me to cover me. I went to the washroom right there. I glanced around to make sure no one else could see me. When I was done, one of my friends said, "Look what you did to

Joey!" I didn't know it, but in looking around, I had squirted Joey by accident. Oh, I'm so sorry...I know I'm wrong."

Next, Joey joined us in the office. Ordinarily, this offence would warrant a suspension; however given the circumstances, we changed gears. We all agreed that Ziggy had make a poor choice. We discussed that if this ever happens again, Ziggy was to find a teacher and if this was not possible, he was to just to go inside the school, and return outside to tell the teacher his reasons later. Ziggy was convinced it would never happen again!! Anyway, I asked the boys if they would like to fix the situation. Ziggy exclaimed still quite upset, "I'll do anything Joey wants."

I asked Ziggy what was the belonging of Joey he had hurt. Ziggy responded, "...his pants." I asked if he could do something to make things right. Ziggy responded, "Well, maybe I could wash them." "Have you ever washed anything?" I asked. "No!" said Ziggy. "Well, could your Mom teach you and allow you to do it yourself?" "I think so," replied Ziggy. I went on to mention that maybe the pants could be ironed, too. Finally, Joey spoke up, "...but they're my favorite pants and we have sleepover at the school tomorrow night!" "Well," I said to Ziggy, "what can you do?" "I could drive them to his house so he would have them for school!" suggested Ziggy. "Good plan," I countered and so it was decided. Joey felt good about his pants and Ziggy felt he had retained a friend.

Both sets of parents were informed and Joey's parents were in full agreement with the decision. I felt that the boys had developed a mutual Restitution plan where both boys could feel strengthened and affirmed.

I Didn't Mean It – Pay Forward

Although the Restitution story above was one that solved the problem in a peaceful way and resulted in a payback it can be enhanced by adding the following. Below is a dialogue between the restitution counselor and the student.

C. I hear what happened and I think it was an accident. But I also think it is something we can learn from. Do you want to do that?

S. Yes.

C. First I want to ask you if you think you could have done worse?

S. (Thinks). Yes if I did it on purpose.

C. I agree that would have been worse. Also would it have been worse if you had just gone on the ground?

S. Yes.

C. Because what's our belief?

S. Respect yourself, others and our mother earth.

C. And you did respect our playground?

S. Yes.

C. So you were remembering our belief? Why did you ask the boys to gather around?

S. So no one would see my privates.

C. So give yourself credit you showed respect and thought about safety. Do you agree?

S. Yes

C. Did your friends gather around when you asked them?

S. Yes

C. What does that say about you?

S. I dunno.

C.   I think you have people who care about you and also they listen when you say something. What do you think?

S.   I think that's right.

C.   One last thing. How did you invent that idea to solve your problem? It was pretty creative to think it up.

S.   But I peed on Joey.

C.   I know. That was one bad part, but there were four good parts. You respected our playground, you kept your privates private, you knew how to get help from your friends and you invented a way you thought would solve the problem.

S.   Yeah.

C.   Are you giving yourself credit? Sometimes a good idea has a small bad side to it. I think you were doing the best you could at the time. Do you think you could talk with Joey and your friends to solve this?

S.   Maybe.

C.   How would it be better for you and how would it be getting yourself stronger.

S.   Maybe I could help some other kids who have this problem.

C.   That's also our part of the problem – that you couldn't find a supervisor to let you in. We teachers need to talk together to solve this and we'll tell you what our part will be to make it better.

S.   Maybe we could have one door open?

C.   Maybe if we can figure our how to be safe too. Do you need a suggestion or help to talk to Joey?

S.   No I know what I'll do. I'll ask his mom if I can wash his pants.

C.   How will it be better for you if you do that?

S.   He'll know I didn't do it on purpose.

RESTITUTION RESTORES RELATIONSHIPS

Restitution is about restoring and strengthening people. It is about helping youth think about who they want to be as individuals and how they want to treat others. Restitution as we use the word is a process of reflection and healing. This process creates safe conditions for people to be honest with themselves and to evaluate the impact of their actions on others. Adults can learn to be intentional about this, to model it for youth. When the healing and self-examination are finished the person who has damaged another desires to repair the hurt relationship to make amends. This is done by the individual trying to be the person he or she wants to be and secondly helping the other or the group. Restitution is self discipline, which is learning about oneself. It is learning to be a moral person and learning to fix one's mistakes. It is done first for oneself and secondly for others. Restitution benefits all involved.

Story: After September 11th

The week following the fall of the world trade center was tense for everyone. In Winnipeg a middle school student said to a Muslim classmate "Go back to your f…ing country." I was phoned by the school about the incident. They told me he had already been suspended for two days, but they wanted to do Restitution with him when he returned to help him improve his attitude. They asked if I thought it would be a good idea to have him study about the country of Pakistan and make a report to share with the students. I said it would be a possibility, but we wouldn't know whether he was doing it to avoid pain, to comply or to be the person he wanted to be. We discussed ways of facilitating an internal change in his perception toward our belief in respect. I asked what nationality the boy was and was told he was from Eastern Europe. I suggested he would have grandparents or aunts and uncles who immigrated to Winnipeg after the Second World War. We decided to invite him to interview them about what it was like to be a new non English speaker in a Canadian school. Then, if he chose to, the boy could share what he learned with his fellow student from Pakistan. This could create a common ground between them. It would be supported by the family. It would be restorative and he would be strengthened as a person.

RESTITUTION IS AN INVITATION NOT COERCION

Restitution can't be coerced. A forced restitution is not a real restitution! It is a consequence. If you force restitution the person will ask you, "What happens if I don't do it?" If they dislike the consequence you propose, the person may comply and agree to repair their mistake, but they do it to avoid being uncomfortable or to avoid the loss of freedom or the removal of a privilege. They may even continue to comply as long as the sanction is held in place. In their minds they believe in "an eye for an eye" and they rationalize that if their hurt to another has resulted in a discomfort for them then things are even. A small child will say, "You can hit me back." to even the score. If we have nothing to hold over their heads they go back to behaving the same as before because they haven't changed inside. This is because the process was not restorative. Forcing restitutions is counter productive to moral development which is based on an individual's choice. You can create conditions where the person will want to solve their problem and do better next time if you say, "It's okay to make a mistake. You're not the only one. We've all done things we regret. You can fix it if you decide you want to." This conversation is an invitation rather than a threat or persuasion. It is not "Do it or we'll hurt you." It is, "Do it to grow yourself into a better person."

Story: Am I Being The Nephew I Want To Be?

It's hard to learn to not persuade or threaten youth to do a task. Here is a personal example from my life. I was at Gabriola Island for Easter. My teen son and my nephew were watching my brother, their Uncle Bill, build some steps from the top of the cliff down to the water's edge. I thought about telling them to help him. Actually I thought I'd say to my son, "If you don't want to help around here don't ask me for money to get your car fixed." Reflecting on this I decided that would be setting the scene for him to at best conform to avoid pain. Possibly he would rebel. He'd have no ownership of his effort. Then I thought I'd say, "C'mon Jake, you're such a good guy. Please help your uncle. Do it for me."

Then I self evaluated. Both of these approaches would be attempts to control the boys externally to do what I thought was right. Nothing I suggested was tied to their values. I had not created conditions for them to self evaluate. I thought to myself I should ask them about our family beliefs. I hesitated because I thought they'll think this is so hokey. They'll say, "Don't use that psychology on us." Then I decided that if I believed in restitution I needed to be practicing what I spoke about. I took a deep breath.

I said, "I know this might sound like psychology but I want to ask you a couple of questions." Then I said, "What do we believe in our family about sharing the work load? What do you see your dads and uncles do when we're building a cottage at the lake? What do we moms do when we prepare a meal together? How do you guys share responsibility when you room together?" The hardest part of the conversation was to keep guilting or cajoling from my tone. I said to the boys, "Don't answer me. Think about it for yourself. Whatever you decide is up to you." I meant it. I had created the context for self evaluation. I had been the parent I wanted to be. I had to have a little faith in our modeling and their values.

I deliberately walked back to the house. As I watched their non-verbals out the window, I was wondering would they slouch over in a whipped manner to offer their help. If so, I knew their feeling would be resentment at being coerced or would my son come in, put his arm around me and say placating, "I'll do it for you Mom"? Neither of these happened. They talked for about ten minutes and then they sauntered over to where their uncle was working and conversed with him.

The next thing I saw was my son up in a harness over the water. The boys worked for two and a half hours, joking with each other as they went. They called us over at four o'clock to show us their work, proud of their achievement. They asked for no monetary compensation. Nor did they even need our praise. They had been the nephews they wanted to be—at least for that day.

RESTITUTION TEACHES THE PERSON TO LOOK INSIDE

In Restitution we help people see the incongruity between how they behave and who they want to be. Once we have offered the invitation for self-healing to the person we can ask them the following questions to help them to focus internally.

- What kind of person do you want to be?

- What would it look like, sound like, and feel like if you were being that kind of person?

- What do you believe about how people should treat each other?

- How do you want to be treated when you make a mistake?

- What is your family value on this topic? Do you hold this value?

- If not, what do you believe? Can I talk to you about it?

If we are doing something to hurt someone else we can ask our higher self. If we can reach that part of us it will tell us the answer. If we wonder if someone is telling the truth we can ask that part of our self for the answer.

Does this mean that we espouse a narcissistic view? Do we want a child who says, "me first", "mine", "I will have it", all the time? No, we do not. Nor do we want youth to be so accustomed to compliance that when we ask them, "What kind of person do you want to be?" they quickly say, "Sorry" without self evaluating what they have done. When we ask, "How do we want to treat each other in the class?" we don't want them to search our faces to find the answers we want to hear. When we ask, "Is it okay to make a mistake and they hang their heads and say, "No, I was bad." When we ask, "What can you do to fix it?" We don't want them to choose something to do as a reparation that is demeaning rather than self-strengthening.

Sometimes the child looks guilty. I think the child has learned elsewhere to feel guilty. If we see that on his face we quickly say something like, "It's okay to make a mistake. No one is perfect. You can fix it!" And he does.

Self evaluation is developed by clearly thinking about who you want to be and being vigorously honest about what you are actually doing. We can teach youth to do this if we can create a climate free of fear or defensiveness so that they can reflect. We also have to withhold our judgement in order for these youth to make their own evaluation rather than just telling us what we want to hear.

After the person has explored who they want to be we can then ask a question about the problem such as, "How often does it happen? Where were you?" or, "Exactly what did you do?" They will not lie to us. They don't need to be defensive because they know we all make mistakes and help each other fix them.

"Don't answer me. Answer yourself. One can't change one's life unless there is honesty inside." We do not initially ask the person to label their behavior right or wrong. If they do so spontaneously it is all right, but we don't want to comment on what they say. Let them sit with it and reflect upon their actions, even if they are very young.

Story: Look Inside and You Will Know the Answer

A principal in Washington State told me a story about her four-year-old daughter. They had been out hiking and while she ran up the last hill herself, her daughter decided to stop and draw a picture. When her mother returned the picture was held up for inspection. The mom was tired and gave it a perfunctory inspection upon which her child challenged her. She said "Mommy, how come you just said 'um' to me?" "What do you mean?" asked her mom. The daughter replied "Usually you say 'Oh Aune, this is so sweet. I really love it, keep up the good work!' Chagrined, my colleague repeated all the words her daughter wanted to hear and the child smiled and was satisfied. However, the exchange raised the mom's consciousness of how her daughter had become dependent on her positive reinforcement. She realized she had taken on the responsibility for passing judgment rather than leaving Aune in self evaluation.

As a result of this interchange she had a further conversation. She said, "Who really knows if this is a good picture Aune? Who knows how much time and thinking you used to make it?" Aune replied "I don't know. No one saw me do it." The mom then asked, "Who is the person who saw this picture all the time you were doing it?" When Aune looked perplexed she answered, "You Aune are the only one who knows. What do you think of your picture? What do you like about it? Would you do anything different the next time? Was anything hard to do?" This helped Aune moved onto self evaluation. She was delighted as she talked about why she had made her picture. This is the strengthening piece.

If children can self evaluate their motivation when they do well, it will not be threatening to do so when they have problem. If the only time we ask them to self evaluate is when they make a mistake, they may become wary. Also to self evaluate in the presence of error is the most difficult because they may be fearful and not thinking. Restitution is a pull system not a push system. When we push we remain the monitor watching from outside. We are taking responsibility for the behavior of the kids. If we help kids develop new internal pictures, these pictures will organize their behavioral system from the inside out. The question is to identify how we can invite students to take in new pictures. A start is through our relationships. If they take in to their heads one of us as a need-satisfying person they'll take in some of our pictures and values.

RESTITUTION IS ABOUT LOOKING FOR THE BASIC NEED BEHIND THE PROBLEM

To move from self evaluation to self restitution it is important for a person to be able to recognize the impact of their actions on others. Learning that all people have basic needs of Love, Power, Freedom, Fun and Survival will greatly assist this process. Youth with these tools, are almost always able to identify what need of the other person's they have disrupted by what they have chosen to do. They also will be able to identify what need was behind their own behavior. Once they have these tools it is easy to move to self restitution. Moving the discussion away from fault to focusing on the needs of both parties immediately reduces responses which are merely combatative. In Restitution we talk about collapsing conflict. This is a process by which we identify each person's need and then invent a solution that works for all.

To teach the needs ask youth to look inside and read their feelings. Sad and lonely feelings tell us we have an unmet love need. Angry, fighting feelings tell us our power need is rising. The feeling of being pushed, suffocated or overloaded is usually signalling a lack of freedom. Fear or being tired, hungry or cold tells us we feel unsafe. Boredom signals a lack of fun. When life becomes too serious we aren't generous to ourselves or to others. We can't laugh at ourselves and we aren't creative. When I teach Glasser's Basic Needs circle up North they tell me it is the medicine wheel. They name the needs belonging, mastery, independence, and generosity.

When students learn to identify their needs instead of staying on the bad feeling they can first ask for help and then learn to get what they need.

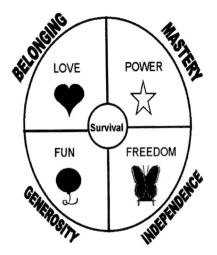

Students are taught to view their negative feelings as signals that tell them which need is not being met. They have their feelings and they verbalize their feelings, but they don't dwell on them. As soon as a child has articulated a feeling, the teacher helps to identify whether this feeling signals a need for love (belonging), power (mastery), freedom (independence), fun (generosity), or safety. Children know their restitution plans must include provisions for them to meet their own needs without violating others needs. The following is letter I received from a teacher.

Diane, I wanted to update you on an experience I had. I did remember you saying to me that day how important it is to teach the needs to students. I had been hesitant to do that because I really didn't believe the age and population of students I work with would "get" it. I am a Physical Education teacher with behavior disorder students, age four to sixteen. I decided if you said it, it must be true, and set a goal for myself for this school year to do that with them.

We finally got around to it the beginning of October. Wow! What a great experience. We continue to do activities around our needs every couple weeks at the beginning of class. My students are so into identifying their needs when they have a problem. It has really helped to get the kids through problem times much more quickly and with better understanding on their part. Two of the more touching experiences I've had I would also like to share with you if I could take a little more of your time.

After introducing each of the needs I showed the kids the pictures we were going to use to represent them. When we got to the star for power I asked why they thought a star was used. Since we had talked about how power represents things we are good at I was thinking they might say, "Teachers give stars when you do good stuff or something." One of my students, who can really be a challenge at times, said, "I think the reason we have a star for our power need is that stars shine bright in the sky, and when we are meeting our power need we are shining bright like the stars." So that is my new explanation for power.

My other story happened just the other day. One of my students came in with his head hanging down. When I asked if there was something bothering him he said, "I broke my love need. I've been thinking about when my Dad had heart surgery and almost died. I need help fixing it." So I helped him come up with some happy thought about his dad which was that he was coming to see him on the weekend. When the teacher came to get him he told him how he fixed his need for love, and was very proud of it.

In the example above the children are young ones. In the following story you will recognize that the high school students have been taught about their basic needs.

Story: I Don't Want To Be A Violent Person

A seventeen year old youth had been seeing the counsellor regarding personal and relationship concerns. Among the identified issues that had deeply affected his life was the physical abuse that he and his mother had suffered at the hands of his father…ultimately leading to the need for the mother to move to another province with her children, seeking refuge in a shelter for abused families. Roy's mother subsequently moved to another city. Roy missed his mother a lot and was delighted when arrangements were made for him to go visit her over a school holiday. Upon his return, he came to see the counselor, very distraught about how things had evolved. Roy's mother was in a new relationship with another man. The first few days had gone okay, but Roy was kicked out following an altercation with his mother's boyfriend, which had resulted in Roy beating up the boyfriend. Roy felt terrible.

C: Looks like things didn't turn out the way you wanted. I can see you're feeling bad. Do you want to talk about it?

R: I got into a fight with my mom's boyfriend and I beat him up...I shouldn't have done that...You know I don't like violence...that makes me just like my dad.

C: One thing we've talked about is that nobody's perfect and we all make mistakes sometime...so don't be too hard on yourself. Do you feel this was a mistake?

R: (Nodded his head) Yeah.

C: Can you tell me what was going on that you fought? What were you wanting?

R: I didn't like the way he was treating my mom...so I got mad and made him stop. I love my mom. I want her to be safe.

C: So how do you want your mother to be treated?

R: With respect...when I was a kid I couldn't help her...

C: So now that you're older and bigger, you can protect yourself and your mom....So should I tell you not to want your mom to be safe or respected?

R: No!!!!

C: I agree...So wanting to protect your mom is a good thing...You've also talked about the kind of person you want to be...tell me what kind of person you want to be?

R: I don't want to hurt other people...I hate that!!

C: So if we could figure out a way for you to stand up for yourself and your family, without being a violent person, would that be worth talking about?

R: Yes, but I'm going to need help.

The next day Roy brought in his girlfriend. They revealed to the counselor that they were fighting and that he was allowing her to hit him. The counselor helped them identify their needs. He was accepting her punishment because he loved her and wanted the relationship. She was hitting him because it gave her a sense of power that she never had when she was as a child abused verbally and physically by her brother. Once they understood the needs behind their behavior, they both felt ashamed so their counselor had to stabilize them.

C: Should I tell you not to care about this relationship?

R: (Shook his head.)

C: So is it important to have love?

R: (He nodded.)

C: Tough as you've had it give yourself credit you haven't given up on love.

Then the counselor talked to the girl.

C: Should I tell you Annette not to stick up for yourself?

A: (Shook her head.)

C: So is it important to have some power and control in your life?

A: (Nodded.)

C: Would it be better to let people walk all over you?

A: No.

C: So if you could figure out a way to assert yourself and show respect for Roy would you do it?

A: (Nodded tentatively.) I won't hit him anymore.

C: I won't do it again is not the only answer. You still have to have a plan so you can have some self power. Do you think it's going to be easy?

A: It will be hard.

C: But do you still want to do it?

A: (Smiled) Yes, because I love Roy.

C: So let's begin to talk about how you can help each other get what you need in a loving healthy way. How can you have some control (power) and be connected (belonging).

SELF RESTITUTION IS THE MOST POWERFUL TOOL

Self restitution teaches a person to move from commenting on others to commenting on their own actions because of the realization that one can only control oneself. Dr. William Glasser says, "Happy people evaluate themselves, unhappy people evaluate others." Self restitution is about evaluating oneself. Self restitution involves three steps. The first step is to say, "I don't like what I did. I was not the friend, student, teacher, etc. that I want to be." The second step is to pick up a piece of the problem and say what one's part of the problem has been. The third step is to verbalize what will happen next time so the relationship will be better. When one is able to self restitute one gains a greater sense of control and purpose.

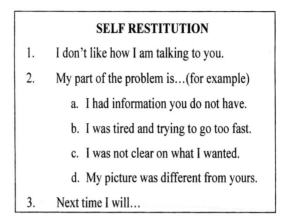

SELF RESTITUTION

1. I don't like how I am talking to you.

2. My part of the problem is…(for example)

    a. I had information you do not have.

    b. I was tired and trying to go too fast.

    c. I was not clear on what I wanted.

    d. My picture was different from yours.

3. Next time I will…

As we teach staff members to self restitute, relationships are strengthened among teachers. As adults model self restitution for youth they move from a "toe to toe" adversarial position to standing "shoulder to shoulder" cooperating with the youth. Staff feel less judged, more accepted and take greater ownership of their problems and the challenge of finding solutions.

Story: I Don't Like The Way You're Talking To Me

I used to say to my daughter. "I don't like the way you're talking to me." Since I was modeling evaluating her rather than myself, I frequently heard a comment from her in which she evaluated me. For example she would say "Well I don't like the way you're talking to me either." My how well I taught her! I thought about how I might change my comments and the next time I approached her I said "I don't like the way I'm talking to you. This is not the mother I want to be." She responded "Well I wasn't talking too nicely to you either, mom." Nine times out of ten if you self evaluate, the other person will self evaluate. One time out of ten they will use your self evaluation as an opportunity to punish you. For example my daughter might have said "You sure are a witch today." If the person does this try asking them "Would you rather punish me or do you want to make this situation better? Just give me an idea of the direction you want us to go." Having done part one of self restitution with my daughter, I wanted to analyze my part of the problem. I told her it was that I was trying to talk with her when I was too tired. Then I moved to the solution which was a suggestion that we both sleep on the problem and tomorrow try to solve it so we could both get some of what we needed. She agreed and hugged me. Now we were shoulder to shoulder instead of toe to toe.

RESTITUTION IS ABOUT "BEING" NOT "DOING"

If you decide to practise self restitution you will notice that you make an internal shift from focusing on doing to focusing on being. Instead of asking, "What is he or she doing?" you begin focusing on yourself asking, "What am I doing?" Then you begin asking yourself, "Who am I being?" It is an amazing shift because you can be totally present in the moment instead of trying to predict how your actions will affect others or focusing on how you look to them. If you can behave the way you want to be, especially under pressure, you will be satisfied. It is very freeing and also empowering. If your goal includes helping others you will achieve more belonging with self restitution. It can also be enormous fun to discover what you will create to say or do when you focus on being your best self rather than on pleasing others.

When we are helping students with this concept we say things like, "I'm not so concerned about what you did today, instead let's talk about how will you be in the gym tomorrow" or "You can say sorry if you want to but most people want to hear how it is going to be better next time" or with a small child casually ask, "If you do that what does it say about you? or "Is that the kind of friend you want to be?"

Story: Family Vignette

Learning restitution can be fun and playful. When I was in Norway I taught my nephews the three reasons people behave. They had great fun with the idea. The fifteen-year-old said to the eleven-year-old, "Why are you clearing the table Kristofer? Are you doing it so you won't get in trouble (avoid pain)? Are you doing it so we will compliment you and say what a good boy you are (respect from others)? He asked in a teasing manner, or "are you doing it to be the person you want to be?" Kristofer thought and then answered emphatically, "It's my job, I always do my job (respect of self)."

The other night at supper I asked my niece, "Why are you whipping the potatoes? So your mom won't be mad? To please her? For yourself?" She answered, "The middle one," and then she added, "And the last one." She turned and looked at me intently saying, "This could give a whole new perspective on things." I told her, "I'm going to interview you in a month to see what you have to say about what you are learning." I find that it's sometimes hard to start the conversation but always worth the risk!

I am working these days to understand my own behavior and to help my family members understand theirs. If my son says to me, "I don't do guilt, Mom", I self evaluate my tone. Have I been shaming him, creating conditions for him to behave to avoid pain? If so, I say, "You're right, I was guilting you and I'm going to stop because only you can decide what to do based on what you believe is right for you. Sometimes I self evaluate and say, "I don't think I was guilting you. Are you doing it to yourself?" If so, I wonder if he is out of line with his own beliefs?

RESTITUTION STRENGTHENS

How can having a bad situation be a good thing? We all know the answer. A bad situation can be a good thing if we learn from it and get stronger. What does stronger mean to you? It was one of the hardest questions I have been asked when someone said, "You are always talking about stronger, what do you mean by this?" I ask you this question now, "What does stronger mean to you?"

Kids might answer "Muscles." Sometimes they say, "When I can beat them up." They mean strong as aggressive wanting to control others. Adults more frequently say, "When I can control myself." The problem with the latter is sometimes they use the word "control" when they mean repress. We use control to mean manage as "in control." Stronger is not about pushing feelings down. When we are doing this we are overriding valuable signals that we are receiving. Our emotions are always telling us if what we are getting is what we want and need. Strong is having the feeling, realizing what you can change and changing it. What can you change in yourself? How can you change? Get information, learn it, try it, and see yourself applying it successfully. Then you will be strong. Strong, as we mean it, has to do with learning and creating new pictures of how to be.

Some of the things you can say to youth to help them are:

- How will that get you stronger?
- What have you learned that you didn't know before?
- If it doesn't make you stronger it isn't restitution
- Can you make yourself stronger and help the group?
- What's the strong side of your weakness?
- How can you be strong, stick up for yourself and not be violent?

Story: A Cold Day

Two high school girls in a rural area pulled a fire alarm in the school on a cold winter day. As a result of this decision the school was evacuated. There was a nursery in the basement and all the toddlers had to be wrapped up and hurried outside. Although no one was injured, it was a real inconvenience. When the girls were confronted they felt chagrined and asked if they could work in the nursery as a restitution. However the child care workers didn't want the girls so the school phoned me to brain storm solutions. I talked to them about approaching the incident as a learning opportunity. In restitution we believe a misbehavior is pointing us to where a youth needs to learn. Over the phone we walked through this incident.

I asked about the motivation of the girls. One girl we'll call Darlene said she thought it would be fun to pull the alarm. The teachers told me Darlene was always doing crazy things without thinking. I asked what they thought was the life lesson she needed to learn? They decided it was probability determination, thinking ahead how her actions would impact others.

With regard to the second girl, Laura, they said she knew it was wrong but didn't want her friend to be angry with her so said nothing. It was decided that Laura needed to learn to stand up to her peer group. They needed to stress to her the importance to her of friendship and fun and not ask her to sacrifice those needs but to add new skills of assertion.

We decided the teachers would manage the restitution conversation, by asking these girls to reflect on what they could learn that would strengthen them in future situations. The conversations went very well. The girls each realized that a self restitution would involve them telling their parents and the staff their parts of the problem, what they had learned and what they would do when faced with a temptation in the future. The girls were insistent on wanting to do something for the daycare so they asked and were granted the opportunity to spring clean the nursery on a weekend. They felt strengthened by their decision. They could hold their heads high and their parents were proud of them.

If the girls had only cleaned the daycare it would have a been a payback. However, the focus would still have been on making the reparation to please others or to avoid the pain of recriminations. When we move to a restitution pay forward, the focus is solidly on validating at least one good part of the person's misbehavior. At the same time we ask them to recognize a potential strength to meet that need another way. So, for example, Darlene pulled the alarm for fun so we need to say, "Should I tell you it's not important to have fun?" She would say, "No!" Then we can say, "Keep having fun. It's a great part of your personality, but have fun in a way that no one gets hurt."

When talking to Laura we need to ask "Should I tell you it's not important to keep your friends." When she answers "No," we can then say "Would it be getting you stronger if you could keep Darlene as a friend and stand up to her when you know something is wrong?" Laura may say "But it's not possible." We then need to ask "But if it were possible would you want it?" If she says yes we can add "Do you think it's going to be easy? It won't be, but together we can work it out so you can take a life lesson out of this cold day."

The following dialogue illustrates how the teacher questioned them about the weekend cleaning. "Girls, I understand you have agreed to clean the daycare. I have some questions I want to ask you. What are you going to be thinking as you clean this? Are you going to be saying to yourself 'That old bag – she's making me do that?' Will you be feeling guilty and wanting to please us or your parents? Or will you be saying, 'It's ok to make a mistake. We can fix it and it's going to be even cleaner than before! You see, girls, it's not so important what you do as it is what you are thinking when you do it. Only the last way strengthens you. If you aren't getting stronger, it isn't restitution."

The issue was not so much what the girls would do as it was how they would feel while they were doing it. If they were resentful, they were doing it to avoid pain. If they felt guilty they were doing it to please us. If they were in a restorative position they were doing it because they desired it for themselves to make amends to get stronger.

Now when someone says to me, "I'll do it for you", I no longer say, "Thanks, you're the greatest." I tend to say, "Decide if it's worth doing for yourself. Why would you want to do it?" or "If you do it what would you be saying about yourself?" and then I smile. Restitution is playful.

I am sure I could become obnoxious. Fortunately because I'm a normal human being sometimes I also say, "Do it for me." At times I still hear myself say, "Didn't you say you'd do it?" or even, "Do it if you want, but I won't be happy!" The difference now is that I recognize those statements are very controlling. I can stop, reflect, and reframe my words a better way. I can make a restitution for myself when I am not being the person I want to be. As I now operate less in pain for not being perfect and less dependent on approval from others to affirm I'm a good person, I am happier, I am healthier, and I am more in control of my life.

The reason we are successful in permanently lowering incidents of discipline in our schools is that every time a student makes a restitution they enhance themselves. They know more, they see themselves doing things differently and they understand that the impact of their actions on others can be beneficial as well as powerful. This part sets Restitution apart from discipline programs which aim not to strengthen but to induce compliance or to elicit chagrin. Restitution frees youth to choose a better way. Their plans involve learnings they can use over and over in the future.

RESTITUTION FOCUSES ON SOLUTIONS

Restitution focuses on fixing problems, on the solution. We stabilize the student's identity using statements such as "We don't want to focus on blame" or "I'm not so interested in what went wrong as in how we can make it right." Sally Peterjohn, a middle-school teacher in Eden Prairie, Minnesota says she gives the students the "Fab Five." Holding up her hand she counts off on five fingers saying, "I'm not interested in blame, shame, fault, apologies, or excuses." Then she slaps her palm and adds, "I'm only interested in fixing." When her students see her hold up her hand they do not think this means, "Talk to the hand." It means self evaluate.

In my early teaching I wanted my children to admit that their behaviour was not acceptable. But if all behaviour is purposeful, whatever else they were doing had to be need fulfilling for them. The approach I now use is to say, "What was more important? What was your need?" and I seek the underlying cause of a problem.

When a student doesn't have their homework done I suggest teachers ask, "What was more important than doing your homework?" The answers the students give always reveal what need they were controlling for they usually say they wanted to be involved in sports, or TV or talking to a friend. No matter what they answer the teacher can say, "Should I tell you it's not important to do sports, watch TV, etc." The student quickly says, "No."

Developing The Moral Sense

Then she says, "I agree, sports are important. If you could figure out how to do sports and get your homework done, would you?" The person may say it's not possible. If this happens the teacher needs to say "But if it were possible to have both, would you want it?" The student will usually answer "Yes." Then the teacher agrees, "That's what I want too." She asks "Is that what we have to figure out?" "Yes" at this point means we'll have reached another point of agreement. This is a fail safe way to approach conflict. Listen for their need, validate it, then add on our need and collapse conflict.

Ask questions in a non-judgmental manner, such that the individual can evaluate their own behavior non-defensively. Restitution looks for the answers "no" <u>and</u> "yes" to the question "Is it working?" It says, "Help the students also understand why what they did was not good for others, but was need-fulfilling for them at the moment. We do not expound on the uselessness of the child's misbehavior. Without the understanding that all behavior is purposeful, it is almost guaranteed that the plan for restitution will be one where the students merely control themselves and repress their needs. They will say, "Okay I'll just shut up in class" or "Alright I'll sit still." These are not long term solutions because only the teacher's need is met. The students' needs for power and freedom are not met. Here's a story from Dr. Judy Anderson showing how restitution helps strengthen:

Story: Broken Glasses

Two boys came to the office after recess with a bent pair of glasses with the lenses missing. They were upset and still arguing about who did what. When the principal picked up the glasses and asked, "Tell me about the broken glasses," they both started talking at once. The second grader told her how the third grader had hit him in the head, knocking off his glasses and breaking them. The third grader complained about being teased because his team had lost in football. He wants the principal to talk to the three other kids who stepped on the glasses and broke them. He insisted, "I didn't break his glasses. I just pushed him."

The principal reminds the boys, "At our school it's okay to make a mistake. I'm not so interested in who did what to whom, but I am interested in what you want to do about these broken glasses." She puts the glasses between the boys and told them to figure this out while she continues her work. She quickly moves to the other side of the office, turns her back to the boys and purposely starts making some phone calls to break the silence and give them some privacy. After a couple of minutes of silence she hears them arguing about who did what. That ends with another period of silence. Then she hears one of them say, "What do you think we should do about the glasses?" As he picks up the glasses the second boy moves closer. He says, "We're still on the problem we have to get on the solution." They both start bending the frames back in place. The principal doesn't hear the entire conversation, but as they talk their voices became calmer and then more excited.

By the time they come to the principal with a plan they are friendly to each other and enthusiastic about fixing the problem. They say, "We have a plan. We are both involved, so we're both responsible for fixing the glasses." She plays the devil's advocate. She teases the boy with the broken glasses, "Why would you pay for half the repair costs when he hit you in the head and broke your glasses?" He jumps to his friend's defense and tells her how he had repeatedly taunted the boy who hit him about losing the football game, even after he knew the boy was getting angry and had asked him to stop teasing several times.

Then the principal turns to the other boy and challenges him, "I thought you wanted me to talk to the other three boys who stepped on the glasses and broke them. It wasn't your fault; it was their fault! They should pay for the glasses." He assures her that the glasses had fallen on the ground because he had pushed the boy. The three boys that stepped on the glasses had not even known what they had done because it had happened when the bell rang to end recess and all 150 students were rushing inside.

At this point the principal smiles to herself thinking about how things had shifted. Now they were accepting responsibility and honestly talking about their part of the problem. The other shift was in how they felt about each other. This was demonstrated by the other part of their plan that was that the two of them wanted to go outside and try to find the lenses. As soon as they got outside, they got down on their hands and knees. After crawling around for a few minutes they found one unbroken lens. The principal is so encouraged she joins the search, but after 10 minutes they still couldn't find the other lens. She is more skeptical than the boys who are still hopeful and suggest that their whole class might find the other missing lens at their next recess. Sure enough—the two boys come to the office at the end of the day to show her the second recovered unbroken lens.

At dismissal the principal asks the boys, "What are you going to tell your parents?" She smiles, "Are you going to say, 'It wasn't my fault! I shouldn't have to pay.'" They assure her they would explain their part of the problem, and how they solved the problem. The next day, the father of the boy with the broken glasses calls to thank the principal. He was impressed by the enthusiasm of the boys to solve this problem. He was surprised and pleased to tell her that the optician had reassembled the glasses at no cost.

This story is an example of what happens when discipline is taught to students and they are stabilized so their brains can find a solution.

1. The boys had been able to work quite independently to find a solution.
2. The relationship between the boys was strengthened.
3. Each had learned a better way to manage their future behavior.
4. The class had participated in the solution.
5. The parents were validating the school expectation of moving toward self discipline and healing.

In this example, what need do you think the principal was meeting by teasing? We think it was fun but it could also have been belonging.

In the glasses story the student who hit could have done worse by deliberately being destructive (more aggressive) and then denying doing it (more passive). What need do you think he was meeting? We think he needed power because what the second grade student said diminished his power. By refusing at first to cooperate, what worse outcome do you think they were avoiding? We think each was avoiding being in the wrong because they were blaming each other.

Developing The Moral Sense

By deciding to cooperate what need do you think they were meeting? This met their belonging need and by both being successful they had power through a win-win solution. (Belonging and Power). We call this collapsing conflict.

What worse possibility were they avoiding by deciding to solve the problem? The principal would have had to give them a consequence because fighting is serious. How do we know the boys are getting stronger? They begin jumping to each other's defense and focusing on the solution together as a team.

RESTITUTION RESTORES ONE TO THE GROUP

Rather than singling students out as bad examples, there is an attempt to help them save face. In one junior high school using Restitution two students are sent to accompany a removed student back to the classroom. The student is reminded that he or she is part of us and that we want them to be with us. They don't have to slink into the room or arrogantly strut in to show they don't care.

We have a history of excluding children to overcome. We can still see these practices. Where does this all start? When a small child misbehaves we say, "Go out of the story circle'. When they fool around at their desks we say, "Sit on the beanbag chair at the back of the room." When they kick the wall we say, "Go in the hall." When they run up and own the hall we say, go to the office. They are getting older. Pretty soon we say go home for the day.

After a few times we say, "You're out for the semester." There's not much to do in a small town in the winter. If a teen disobeys his parents' rules, they say "You're out of my house." If the teen hits the streets in the big city they are exploited, physically or emotionally. They're now apart from us. We have solved our problem, for the moment. But when we push them away from us we can't teach them. If they won't let us teach them, they can't learn a better way. If they can't learn a better way where will they be for us in the next generation? We have been in a 'dissing' cycle pushing our youth further and further away from us. In the U.S.A. there are more than two million inmates in the prisons. In the year 2000 the budget for corrections in California eclipsed the budget for education. Is this the direction we want to go?

When I worked in Iceland they said, "In a small fishing village we can't push our young men away, we need them to fish for the next generation." They told me that they had words for restitution in their 1000 year old language as well as restorative practices. Some people today have the illusion our youth are dispensable. They are not. Each young man on the street corner is a lost resource. Each inmate incarcerated is a lost opportunity for restorative justice and for reparations to contribute to society.

We have put our young people in destitution – apart from what we have set up rather than practicing restitution – returning them to our social constitution. This is not restorative, this is punitive. Every culture has processes for healing and restoring. The story of Mary Magdalen is illustrative, as is that of the prodigal son. Both were raised up back into the group. When youth are pushed out of the group it makes it easy for them to disconnect from us. They take the picture of other people being need-satisfying out of their world. This leaves them without empathy.

Story: It's Not Just A Toy

The teacher was absent the day that Rashawn, a middle school student, was brought to the office by the paraprofessional because she learned from Jess that Rashawn had threatened Jess in the bathroom with a toy gun. When Rashawn had the gun pointed at the back of Chris' neck, Jess had not known it was a toy. Later, the paraprofessional had learned that Rashawn had been bragging about his ability to potentially hurt Jess. Also, two other students had dared Rashawn to bring a gun to school when Rashawn had threatened that "This would show Jess." The principal approached Rashawn with a calmness characteristic of the climate of respect referred to in the school's constitution. Rashawn's sixth grade class had been one of the first in the school to move toward Restitution but the principal knew from talking with the teacher that Rashawn had not participated in the Restitution process as much as other students. The principal wanted the student to be successful and knew it might take some time. The principal had the initial goal of helping Rashawn to understand and think about what he could do and to create a stronger bond with the school.

"Rashawn, before I talk to you about why you are here (in the principal's office) I want to talk with you about what we think is important at our school. We think it's important for students to know that it's okay to make a mistake, the most important thing is to try to fix it. Is it important to you to know this?" Rashawn shrugged his shoulders without looking at the principal. The principal reminded Rashawn "We are not interested in blame or judgment, we're interested in finding a way to fix what happened so everyone is safe and can learn at our school." The principal explained the discipline code and reiterated the administration's role in bottom line behavior. Rashawn knew he would receive a consequence because bringing a weapon or anything resembling a weapon was a bottom line offense in the school warranting a suspension. The principal then asked Rashawn to see Dr. Grumley, the Restitution counselor, to decide if he wanted to repair the relationships with the school when he returned after the suspension. He didn't have to do it if he didn't want to.

The Restitution counselor asked, "If you chose to fix your mistake, what would that say about how important you thought it was for everyone to be safe in the school so they, and you, could learn?" Rashawn said, "It would show safety was important to me." "Is safety important to you?" "Yeah." "Do you know what you could do to fix the mistake of doing an unsafe act that keeps students from learning?" "Yeah." "What?" "Don't get in trouble any more." "Okay, but you didn't do that for no reason. What could you do so you didn't get in trouble and students are safe and are able to learn?" "I don't know." "Would you want my help, or do you want to try to fix it on your own?" "You can help me." When Rashawn returned after his suspension he and the Restitution counselor came up with three possible options that were presented to the principal.

1. After involving his parent Rashawn would speak to the school about safety and learning during the morning announcements over the PA system.

2. Rashawn could do a presentation to his class about safety that would involve him making a visual aid and working with his teacher.

3. Rashawn would be willing to talk to the victim and those who dared him in order to teach them what he had learned and be available for future occasions when he could be an advocate for safety and learning if others misbehaved.

When the Restitution counselor and Rashawn went to the principal and presented the options the three of them decided on one option with elements from all three: Do a classroom presentation that would involve the parents, for affirmation and assistance in preparing a visual aid, and involve the three other students including Jess. At the end of the week after his teacher had helped him during lunch hour Rashawn made a presentation to the class about safety and learning. Jess and the other two boys who dared him to bring the toy gun also participated, and they created a buddy system to help others that might need to know how to fix problems. This example of the Restitution process demonstrates that working with the student was more important than the product of either "doing time" for a consequence or the written plan. "Working with" students is consistent with the beliefs of the school: to be respectful and responsible. It is also inclusive.

- What could Rashawn have done worse?
- What need was he meeting with the toy gun?
- Could the students have done worse?
- What need were they meeting by reporting to the staff?
- Could the principal have done worse?
- What did he do to avoid this?
- How did the resulting plan meet needs?

We can't motivate children to be kind; we can only create conditions for them to self evaluate by looking inward. We need to help them learn to solve problems without us persuading them to behave. We need to focus on returning the child to the group strengthened rather than time out and suspensions. We talk about how difficult it is to be sure the restitutions strengthen the child. So often when we ask children how to make it right they diminish and deprive themselves. We always say, "If it doesn't get you stronger it isn't restitution."

SUMMARY – WHAT'S A GOOD RESTITUTION?

1. **Repairs** the immediate wrong.

2. **Stabilizes** the person, "It's okay to make a mistake."

3. **Meets the need** of the person hurt.

4. **Focuses** on **meeting the need of the offender.**

5. **Collapses conflict** with a win-win solution.

6. **Explores** what the person could have done worse.

7. **Strengthens** the offenders when they learn new skills.

8. Ties the restitution to the **belief** we've developed.

9. **Returns** the person to the group restoring relationships and offering help or learning to the group.

10. The restitution focuses on how the person is going to **be** more than focusing on what action the person will do.

11. Restitution is **creative** not repetitive. It results in something that wasn't there before.

12. **Redesigns** the system to deal with the presenting problem at its root, the underlying cause.

13. **Evolves** us as human beings – in the best of cases.

Developing The Moral Sense

CHAPTER FOUR
DEVELOPING THE MORAL SENSE

All sects are different because they come from men; morality everywhere the same because it comes from God." – Voltaire

How can one create conditions for a person to develop a moral sense? Children are learning machines. They will seek to experiment with what they see and hear to figure out if it works for them. The old adage, "actions speak louder than words", is relevant here. We adults can ask ourselves, "How are we treating each other? What do our youth see us do? What tone do they hear as we address each other or discuss with others?" Every moment, like it or not, we are modeling for them how people treat each other and how people treat each other is the basis of Restitution.

Restitution is based on the moral judgment individuals freely make about their own behavior when they are free from persuasion, shaming or threats. No one can tell another person how to be self disciplined. One reflects on one's own actions and thinks about how they impact others. Then each of us makes decisions. These decisions lead to actions, which we can then evaluate for ourselves against the intention we desired, and the values we hold. The definition of Restitution is to "Create the conditions for the person to fix their mistakes and return to the group strengthened."

> Create conditions for the person to
> Fix their mistakes and
> Return to the group
> Strengthened

HOW DOES THE BRAIN WORK?

Creating conditions for the development of internal self discipline requires that the individual has time for contemplation. There are three main parts to the brain: the cerebral cortex, the limbic system (mid-brain) and the brain stem (the reptilian brain). Each of these parts has a function. All the parts of the brain interact and influence each other. Energy passes through the brain in the form of biochemical electrical signals. The brain stem is the most primitive part of the brain. We share this structure with all animal forms – even reptiles. This part of the brain controls our involuntary functions. Its job is to maintain temperature, blood pressure, heart rate and the functioning of organs. Among its many jobs it also regulates clamminess of the palms and dilation of the pupils. Its role is survival of the organism. It will function even when a person has severe brain damage.

If we want to create conditions for youth to construct moral meaning, their brain needs to feel safe. Why is this? We humans can perform higher cognitive functions which are seated in the temporal and frontal lobes. Humans have the ability to remember the past and to then apply that information to predict the future. Your dog is not sitting at home depressed about last weekend. Nor is he eagerly anticipating tomorrow. However, a human remembers the impact of his or her actions on others and therefore can understand cause and effect. Humans can recognize patterns, make conscious decisions, use probability determination, plan, and make moral judgments. As information passes through the mid-brain and the limbic system, the amygdalae, which are two small almonds shaped organs on each side of the brain, sense danger. If this happens the incoming energy is diverted to the brain stem. If fear is sensed, adrenaline is released, and then the body gets ready for <u>fight</u> or <u>flight</u>. To understand why one moves to anger we need to understand that at some level the biology of all the strong emotions is the same. Think about it. If your child runs into the road and is almost hit by a car you may be very angry with the child. Why? Because you were terrified, your adrenaline rushed up and externalizing your feelings as aggression gave you a release. Veterans from Vietnam describe the fear of sitting in the jungle all day knowing the Vietcong could be in tunnels beneath them. They released this fearful energy as aggression or as sex when the opportunity arose. We have many people today who are confused in their feelings. One moment they may be crying, the next threatening violence. When we use emotional control on upset people it almost always exacerbates the situation. This also explains why a person says, "I don't do a good performance if I don't have stage fright" or why we see rape following pillage. It explains sadomasochistic practices and kids laughing at drive by shootings. A calm exterior is called for and a deep understanding of what is happening to the upset person at a biological and emotional level.

How can we keep energy flowing to the cerebral cortex so the person we address can understand the pattern? What would prevent this from happening? When a person is angry, fearful, shamed or aroused, the majority of our energy is concentrated on survival. He or she is not making moral judgments about their own actions. They are not even able to discern patterns. An example of this is a person saying, "I know she was mad at me but I don't know what it was about." In other words, one can hear the words but can't pull them together and grasp the pattern to create meaning. When we are downshifted, we can even repeat back what has been said to us but are unable to comprehend or understand the meaning and content of the words. When we don't feel safe, we may seek refuge in rote behaviors, which are stored in our procedural memory, such as pacing the floor or cleaning or rocking. When we frighten, shame, or are angry with children their brains resort to primitive functions and they are incapable of deciphering the moral component of their actions.

People often resort to rote behaviors in times of grief or shock. An example is a woman I had in one of my workshops who said her husband had had a heart attack. When they got to the hospital she was asked what took them so long. Her answer "I had to finish ironing his shirt" shows us she was at the rote level, trying to gain a sense of control and was missing the big picture. Another person told me that he was working the printing press when news came that his mother had died. He said they wanted to send him home, but he said he wanted to stay and finish the printing run to calm himself down. A girl told me about being in an accident and ignoring her injury, focusing instead on finding her barrette refusing to leave till the ambulance attendants had helped her to get it.

Our family had a car rollover, two adults and five children. We were all belted in so we were not hurt, but the window blew out of the back of the car and the doughnuts which had been on the ledge blew all over the road. My aunt got the donut box and started collecting them up from the ditch. Then she started passing them to all the cars which were stopping on the road. As kids we laughed. Now I look at this incident as an example of her brain downshifting to the rote level. "When I'm passing dainties everything is okay" was the program she was running to give herself a sense of order in the midst of chaos.

Think about your experiences. If the doctor gives you bad news your brain will downshift and you won't make sense of the instructions you hear. Feel free to say to your spouse "I am going to take the kids and leave," but understand that there will be so much fear or anger that the person won't hear anything else you have to say. Think now of examples when you know your brain was downshifted.

New information tells us our approach to discipline using brain-based learning will need to be one that does not threaten students. Eric Jensen who has studied the brain extensively says:

> Learners who feel threatened by adults are least likely to change behavior because the part of their brain that deals with "perceptual mapping" and complex behavior change is unable to be engaged. Learners who are constantly threatened, disciplined and bribed with rewards may be unable to work for delayed gratification. The part of their brain they need to use, the frontal lobes, are less likely to be engaged under a system where others have control.[8]

So when we say we have a gut feeling about someone it is true. A baby knows the emotional state of its mother and is finely tuned to sense it. It is normal to sense what other beings are feeling.

> The amygdala [has] a privileged position as an emotional sentinel, able to hijack the brain...sensory signals from eye or ear travel first in the brain to the thalamus, and then –across a single synapse—to the amygdale; a second signal from the thalamus is routed to the

---

[8] Eric Jensen, *Brain-based Learning*. 1996, p.255.

neocortex—the thinking brain...Those feelings that take the direct route through the amygdale include our most primitive and potent; this circuit does much to explain the power of emotion to overwhelm rationality.[9]

Why then does one lose emotional sensitivity and numb out feelings? Why would a child become hyper vigilant? This is what we need to understand in order to raise healthy people.

The higher we are in the perceptual system, the more time the process takes. The lower levels of perception are a faster part of our nervous system. Such an example would be a reflex such as a fight or flight reaction. The other day I caught something that was falling before I even thought about it. I looked in my hand and there it was. This is because my action was at the automatic program level, below conscious thinking, and therefore faster. Thinking about morals and values is at a high level of perception and we need to provide youth with time to reflect. If information can't reach the frontal lobes a person remains at the program level making rote responses, conforming or reacting, without reflecting.

THE BRAIN IS SOCIAL

The brain is social. One can't become a moral person in a vacuum. One needs to converse with others to create personal perspectives and values. Even a monk who meditates in solitude is reflecting on the words and writings of others. When we talk about Restitution we are talking about

---

[9] Daniel Goleman, *Emotional Intelligence: Why It Can Matter More Than IQ.* New York: Bantam Books, 1995, p17.

level six of Lawrence Kohlberg's stages of moral development. At this level one behaves not for societal reasons but because one has developed a moral compass that guides from inside. One can think about the innate propensity of the human to have a moral sense regardless of the culture in which they are reared. This propensity may or may not be realized depending on the conditions created. Here I am in the middle of my life just now beginning to intentionally reflect upon this question: must one be mature to be in touch with one's higher self? I think not. One teacher said to me in a workshop recently, "I think children are at this level before they go to school, before we start to monitor and reward them." Is this developmentally possible? Is there an altruistic caring part of each child which we can nurture and encourage?

James Wilson thinks so. He believes the human has an innate moral sense, a predisposition to be good if we can create the conditions for this moral sense to be manifest and made strong.

> "We have a moral sense, most people instinctively rely on it even if intellectuals deny it, but it is not always and in every aspect of life strong enough to withstand a pervasive and sustained attack....To say that people have a moral sense is not the same thing as saying that they are innately good. A moral sense must compete with other senses that are natural to humans - the desire to survive, acquire possessions, indulge in sex, or accumulate power - in short, with self-interest narrowly defined. How that struggle is resolved will differ depending on our character, our circumstances and the cultural and political tendencies of the day. But saying that a moral sense exists is the same thing as saying that humans, by their nature, are potentially good."[10]

---

[10] James Q. Wilson, *The Moral Sense*. New York: Macmillan, Inc., 1993, p.12.

For a youth to construct morals it is necessary to first reflect then to engage in vigorous dialogue challenging others' perceptions and being asked to support one's own point of view. In Restitution we do this by designing activities where children think about who they want to be and what they believe.

Time For Reflection

A person needs time and space for reflection. Why is space necessary to create moral meaning? Rachael Kessler in *The Soul of Education* says reflection takes time, "Moments of deep connection to the self – when we really know ourselves, express our true self, feel connected to the essence of who we are – nourish the human spirit. Some people define this connection to the self as the bedrock of spirituality, from which all other connections flow …through being alone, we can contact the deeper truth of our natures. Once we are profoundly honest with ourselves, we may see reality (and other people) with greater objectivity and openness."[11]

I used to say sternly to my children and students when they hesitated, "Answer me. I'm talking to you!" Now I say the opposite. I say, "Don't answer me. I'm going to ask you again in ten minutes. Think about it." Sometimes I even say, "I have a question for you. I want you to think about it when you're going to sleep. See if you can figure out an answer. I'll do the same thing tonight and we can talk tomorrow."

---

[11] Rachael Kessler, *The Soul of Education: Helping Students Find Connection, Compassion and Character at School.* Alexandria: Association for Supervision and Curriculum Development, 2000, p. 22.

Developing The Moral Sense

What Can You Do To Fix It?

When I go to schools to talk to teachers about self discipline I ask them "What is the first thing that youth say to you when you ask them, what can you do to fix it?" They always give me the same answer, that students shrug and say, "I don't know." When asked again, their second response is, "I'll apologize." When we say back to the youth, "You have the right to feel sorry. Now what's going to be different the next time?" their third answer is, "I won't do it again." It is important to understand that none of these three answers is Restitution. To get Restitution we must say to them, "That would be need-fulfilling for them but what are you going to do to solve the problem, get yourself stronger, and help the group? What do you need? If you aren't learning to get your needs met you can't help others." If they can figure this out, they are on the road to Restitution.

WHY DO THEY SAY WHAT THEY SAY?

Why do they say what they say? They do what we've taught them to do and they learn it early. Two-year-olds can't learn it because they are too egocentric. Developmentally they are not ready to understand the impact of their actions on others. Their brains are not capable of seeing the pattern nor do they understand cause and effect. So if you say to a two-year-old, "Who did it?" They will proudly say, "I did it." If they spilled something they may even regard it as a work of art. Now, if we say to a three-year-old, "Who did it?" she'll flush but say nothing. She understands she has done something wrong. She knows that spilled ketchup did not go where it was meant to go. She is developmentally ready to know she has made a mistake.

When a child flushes it is a precious moment – a precious moment of self evaluation. She has in her brain a mismatch between what she was aiming for and what she accomplished. Why is this a precious moment? Her flushing shows us her self evaluation system is in perfect working condition. It would be a similar mismatch to that which she would have if she accidentally stepped on the cat's tail. What she wants is for the cat to be comfortable and calm. When she hears the yowl she experiences a bad feeling, a mismatch, which tells her that her action created dissonance. She knows what is right and she can feel what is wrong. Two year old children can feel discomfort, but they don't always know what they should have done so they can't evaluate, "Is what I'm doing getting me what I want?" Three-year-old children are developmentally capable of doing so if we don't mess it up!

How Can We Mess Up a Precious Moment?

We can mess it up by diverting them from looking inside to analyze and solve their problem. We do so by guilting, "Look what you did. I told you not to do that" or by punishing, "You're so bad; you're going to get it." Immediately the child's attention is diverted to our comments and she looks externally to protect herself. She is no longer engaged in internal self evaluation. She is concerned instead about her safety. This concern results in her brain downshifting to fight or flight, and she can't think to solve the problem.

If a child is punished repeatedly, they learn to detach from us so they won't have bad feelings. They don't flush, because they don't care. How can this happen? It happens because they take us and our goals out of their heads.

For example, if a child doesn't care about the cat's comfort the child doesn't flush when she steps on its tail. Some children may learn to detach their emotions so completely that they can dispassionately injure an animal without having the feeling to stop, the error signal that healthy people have. As this child grows up he or she may brutalize humans without feeling. Many veterans report having had this detachment experience in war when required to kill other humans. They did it to survive. So do the children.

WHY WOULD WE CARE ABOUT HOW OUR BRAIN WORKS?

We care if we want our youth to become moral people. Children can only become moral people if they are operating in the front region of their brains. Humans have the ability to future think, make decisions and plan when we have energy going to the front of our brains. When this is happening in the front of our brains, an MRI scan shows yellow with pockets of red activity. When our brains downshift, the brainstem will be displayed in red because it becomes very active. We aren't thinking at this moment, the focus of the system is fight or flight. You can see when a child's brain has down shifted when they give you the "big-eyed" look which means they are frightened, or the "slit eyed" look which means they want to hurt you back.

Think About It

I know when I raised my children I always wanted to see the big-eyed look on their faces. To me this meant I had their attention. What a fool I was! I had their attention, but they weren't thinking. Sometimes I even asked them,

"Are you listening to me?" They could repeat back every word I'd said, even my last sentence, but they weren't thinking. They were using procedural memory which is a band across the midbrain. Rote behavior is happening to a child who tells us what we want to hear to avoid our displeasure. The child may say, "I'm sorry I did this," but doesn't reflect on the words or speak from the heart. In the presence of error, do you want your child to be calm enough to figure out how to fix a problem or do you want them to be frightened with their brains focusing solely on survival?

I can remember when I taught delinquent youth, making the following comment to my co-workers, "Let's scare him up so he knows we're serious." What folly! I could scare him up, but then I couldn't teach him because his brain was downshifted and he was detaching his feelings so as to stay in control. Feel free to shame but understand that if you do so, you are contributing to violence.

What About Four Year Olds

Four-year-old children have learned what we've taught them. When we ask a four-year-old, "Who did it?" "What happened?" They answer, "Did what?" "I didn't do it!" "He did it," "She did it," "The dog did it," or "You made me do it!" Have we taught them that if they flush and say, "I did it," things don't get better? They have learned to hide their mistakes or, even worse, to lie to us. But remember we taught them to do this to avoid discomfort from us. They are looking externally to protect themselves, not internally to self evaluate their actions.

How Can We Help?

Let's go back to the three-year-old child flushing. When we see the flush instead of viewing it as guilt and an invitation to punish we can calm her. We can say, "It's ok to make a mistake," or "You're not the only one," or "We still love you," or "You can fix it." Our goal will be to lift off her fear and guilt so she can keep looking inside to decide what is the right thing to do. Some cultures even pretend not to notice the mistake if the child can fix it herself. However this will not work if the child has learned to guilt or punish herself.

Won't it be wonderful to overhear our four year old children saying, "It's ok baby; you can fix it," to their dollies. How much better it will be than hearing, "Bad baby, no treats for you. You better not do that again or you'll get it." If we do a really good job with our children we will hear them ask, "What do we believe in our family?" we need to learn to use the golden rule without guilt and ask, "Would you like it if someone did that to you? Think about it and tell me later."

I was visiting my four grandchildren in Edmonton when I had a real learning experience. We were getting ready to go to the Edmonton Mall when there was a knock at the door. It was the neighbor who said to my son in law "Your nine year old just sold this cheap plastic toy to my seven year old for five dollars." Joshua, the nine year old, was called and appeared with an eager face thinking it was time to go to the mall. When he saw the neighbor woman with the toy his face paled. Thank goodness I thought. He knows he did the wrong thing. He has a conscience. Then my son in law held the toy in front of his face and said, "Joshua what is this? What did you do?" He did not yell but he was persistent. My grandson's face got tighter and tighter as he froze up. "Oh my gosh, I thought, his brain is downshifting. What can I do?" I was in conflict because I didn't want to be an interfering mother in law, but I did write this book Restitution. When I get stuck like that I always say to myself "Be the best person you can be."

So I went over behind Josh and put my hands on his shoulders. I said to him Josh, "It's ok to make a mistake. You're not the only one in the family who has done something wrong. Grandma, when she was a little girl, took an ice cream bar from the store and had to go back and pay for it. You can fix this." When I said this to Josh the color came back into his face. His eyes filled up and he looked directly at his dad and said "Dad I know I didn't do the right thing. I can take the toy back. I can pay him back for it, I can give him one of my toys." Josh was allowed to solve the problem and then he and his dad had a talk about why it was important to be honest with people.

The best part of this story is what I noticed in Josh the rest of the weekend. He was so grateful for the help he received that he wanted to help his family. "I can buckle in the baby, Mom. I'll carry that package Grandma. I can take Jeremiah to the bathroom, Dad!" He couldn't do enough to contribute and he didn't do it in a subservient fashion. He did it with energy and he did it to give back to the group.

The story could have had another ending, Josh could have been shamed and been punished by having to stay home from the family outing. He would have been angry with us and been embarrassed when he saw the neighbor. He would not have reflected on his actions or had a chance to restore himself. He may have learned to hide his mistakes better. He would not have reflected on the family beliefs.

I have a humorous example from last Christmas when I was with my grandsons. From time to time I would hear Luc loudly call out "What do we believe in our family about violence?" Sometimes there was muttered response from one of his older brothers "No violence", at other times there was silence, but the problem did seem to be resolved. Whether it was because of the reminder to them or whether it was because we adults had been alerted I am not sure. However it was efficient and it did not result in retaliation or blaming. Hopefully it sparked reflection.

This spring my six year old granddaughter came to her mother and told her that one of her brother's friends was using bad language. Her mom suggested she figure out what she could do to solve it. Soon we heard a strong six year old voice from the other room as Kate said, "In our family we don't talk that way. We are kind so you can't do it in our house." Having family beliefs verbalized in the home give youth the strength to speak out. If they were only to say, "Stop saying bad words" it is possible the recipient of the comment would say "make me." Having the authority of the family to call forth and state the positive belief gives the child another respectable option.

We can't motivate people to be kind; we can only create conditions for them to self evaluate by looking inward. We need to help them learn to solve problems without us persuading them to behave. We need to focus on returning the person to the group rather than giving time out, suspensions, or incarceration. We talk about how difficult it is to be sure the restitutions strengthen the individual. So often when we ask people how to make it right they suggest that they deprive themselves. We need to say, "Get yourself stronger and help the group. How can we all get what we need?"

Restitution is an approach aimed at keeping people in the group and helping them become self directed, self disciplined, and self healing. The emphasis is on the person learning.

ASK, DON'T TELL

It is only through asking questions that we can assist youth in developing an internal moral sense. Following is a conversation one might have with a middle or high school class about Restitution. To move into Restitution first ask the students, "Do you want to have teacher controlled classroom or a student controlled classroom? Students will always answer, "A student controlled classroom."

You can agree this is a nice concept. You can even tease them and ask if they know what they are giving up. Will they miss us hovering over them? Can they survive without our corrections? What will happen if we aren't checking the bathrooms or grading their homework? Who will clue in their parents? How will they know how to behave without consequences? Wow, this could be serious. You can have a few laughs. Then you can say, "Well let's try it, but I reserve the right to go back to the teacher control if things are unsafe. You know what that means. We have rules. We have consequences and if you don't do it I do something to you. I would rather help you learn to be responsible for your own learning and your own behavior and your own relationships." Here's a place you could start.

How Do You Want To Be Treated?

"When you have a problem with someone and you go to talk to them how do you want to be treated? Think about it and write it down. When you're finished, talk about what you've written with two or three other people and write down what you all agree on. Let's share with the group when you're done and see where they agree with us. Where is there a difference? Let's talk about it. Finished? Have we got a good list of how we want to be treated when we go to talk to a person with whom we have a problem?"

You Can Decide

"Can you make a person treat you this way? Can you control them? Think about it? Who can you control? Yourself? Are you sure about that? Can you be the person you decide to be? If so, start here. Start with thinking about who you want to be. First think about who you want to be as a friend, then as a student. Talk it over with each other. Now think about the kind of family member you want to be. Brother? Sister? Son? Daughter? Grandchild? Niece or nephew? What do you want to be doing with your family? With your friends? This is called building yourself up from inside out."

Can I Make You Learn?

"Can I make you learn anything you don't want to learn? How might I do it? How could I make this person in our class learn? Give him detention?

Tell him he's going to fail? Pay him? Do you think that might work? It might work for him, but it won't work for me because I'll go broke (smile). How else might I make him learn? Embarrass him in front of the group? Do you think that might work? Or do you think he might embarrass me? What about keeping him from doing sports if he doesn't learn. Do you think that will work? Fail him? I can fail him but will it help him learn? Should I phone his parents? Maybe his mom can make him learn what do you think? Can you think of anything else I can do to make him learn? You can't? Well suppose I do all these things. I have the power. Can I make him or you learn? Think about it. I can't. Learning is something that happens inside you. Becoming a good person is something that happens inside you."

Do You Want To Be Responsible For Your Own Behavior?

"So do you think you are responsible for your own behavior and learning? All I can do is tell you what I will do if your behavior is hurting other people or me. I can't make you learn or do anything you don't want to do. I could spend a lot of time trying, but I'm not going to. I would rather have different conversations. I want to talk about our common goals. Let's move forward and see how it works."

"If someone in our class doesn't want to work this is what I'm going to do. I'll ask, "What are you supposed to be working on? Can I help you get started?" If the person says, "No", I'll say, "If you wanted to do the work could you?" If the person says, "No" I'll say, "I'll get with you when I can" and walk away to get the class started. If the person says, "I could do it but I don't want to." I'll ask, "Are you deciding not to learn today?" If they answer, "Yes", I'll say, "You have the right to sit as long as the other people

Developing The Moral Sense

around you can still do their work." You see I know it's not my job to make anyone learn. It's my job to help those who want to learn." I want to do this and I want to be working with the people who feel good about their jobs."

"We can get the teachers to list their beliefs. We can decide to take strong action where we can. We can get all the teachers to agree that if they see our beliefs hurt they will act on the spot. When you students see teachers upholding the beliefs it makes it easier for you to help your friends. You can say to a bully, "You can't say that. That's harassment. That is not what we do here." We can also work together so no one needs to be failing. Let's send this list to the teachers' staff meeting and see what they think."

ARE YOU READY FOR THE CHALLENGE?

In *Unleashing the Power of Perceptual Change*, Renata and Geoffrey Caine[12] list three kinds of teachers categorized according to their Perceptual Orientation. Perceptual Orientation 1 teacher is a conventional teacher but not a punisher. Perceptual Orientation 2 teacher is in transition, using many approaches such as cooperative learning and thematic instruction but still providing the structure for learning. Perceptual Orientation 3 teacher focuses on wholeness and dynamic learning. They know the importance of self organization. They are invested more in the process than the product. They are self referencing, they understand mindfulness and are not afraid of self disclosure.

---

[12] Renata and Geoffrey Caine, Unleashing the Power of Perceptual Change: The Potential of Brain-Based Teaching, Alexandria: Association for Supervision and Curriculum Development, 1997, p.88.

This last person is the teacher we need to help us move our class management practices into a restorative model which evolves us as human beings. A consequence based discipline is used by a Perceptual Orientation 1 teacher. My book, *Restitution: Restructuring School Discipline* was a transition piece. Perceptual Orientation 2 teachers embraced the new strategies presented therein. Perceptual Orientation 3 teachers who have the brain based perspective are ready to move beyond the structure programs to journey with their students and community to a better way of being.

Using Restitution requires people who are authentic and self reflective and who are willing to practise self restitution publicly so others can learn from their processing.

My understanding of internal motivation came from learning Control Theory. I was presented with these ideas jointly by William Glasser and William Powers when they collaborated on the book *Stations of the Mind* in 1981. From them I came to understand that we control for input, all behavior is purposeful and that we each create our own realities so we must seek to understand how others perceive the world. I will ever be grateful for those teachings. For whole year I repeated to myself, "We control for input; behavior is the control of perception." I began to slowly understand that during my career teaching special education at the university I had focused too much on the behavior and not enough on the intent of the person which was where the control really lay. I began to remind myself, "It's a pull system, not a push system." The ideas of Control Theory now called Choice Theory by Glasser began to meld with my observations from

Aboriginal culture. I experimented and I wrote down what I found in *Restitution: Restructuring School Discipline*.

Restitution is a process structured around the least coercive road which is a way to organize to meet the basic emotional needs of belonging, power, freedom and fun. The freedom need is met in the classes by the teacher asking "Does it really matter?" and using "Yes, If Management" to give youth more choices. The belonging need us met by creating harmony through a class social contract based on the family beliefs of the students. The power need is met through outlining the jobs of the teacher and the jobs of the student. Educators also work with parents to address limits by setting a few bottom line rules to protect the beliefs we've chose. The fun need is inherent in the Restitution questioning process which is creative, and playful. It encourages a generous optimistic view of the world and of our human frailties. In every school which has adopted Restitution incidents of discipline problems have been reduced.

In 1992 when I studied with Peter Senge's Innovation Associates I learned the five disciplines and I realized that change was not merely individual change but it was systemic. My colleague, Judy Anderson and I wrote the book *Creating the Conditions: Leadership for Quality Schools*. In this book we sought to inspire leaders to work in a transformational model with staff. Looking back on this book. I think we were between Perceptual Orientation 2 and Perceptual Orientation 3 in our understanding. In the next chapters I want to review my journey and to share my learnings.

SUMMARY QUESTIONS AND ANSWERS

1. When do kids take responsibility for their behavior?

   When they understand the implications of their actions and when they can construct moral meaning.

2. When will they understand the implications of their actions?

   When their frontal lobes are functioning and they can think about what they have done and how it impacts other people.

3. When will they think about that?

   When they aren't angry or frightened and when their brains aren't downshifted.

4. How will we know they are downshifted?

   Do this in script when they give us the big-eyed or the slit-eyed look.

5. How will we know they are thinking about their responsibility?

   When they flush because they feel guilt internally because they see the pattern of their actions.

6. What has to happen for them to feel guilt?

   They need to be in touch with their feelings to have empathy.

7. When will they have empathy?

   When we stabilize them and when they feel connected to us as a human being.

CHAPTER FIVE

IT'S A PULL SYSTEM, NOT A PUSH SYSTEM

You think because you understand one you must understand two, because one and one
*makes two. But you must also understand **and**.*
An ancient Sufi teaching

Establishing a social contract means the group together creates a shared vision of how they want to be together. This vision pulls us forward with its common purpose. The social contract focuses on beliefs and values rather than on rules. This doesn't mean throw out rules.

We have bottom lines to protect the beliefs. However, a focus on only rules promotes conformity. Beliefs and values tap into internal motivation and promote self discipline. Restitution asks students questions like, "What do we believe?" Do you believe it?" "What kind of a person do you want to be? "How do we want our classroom to be?" It is difficult to answer these questions about beliefs and values if the group hasn't dialogued about them. Stephen Covey states that there are universal beliefs and values that cut across all people, cultures and places, but it's "unexplored territory." Establishing a social contract provides an opportunity for the teacher and students to examine this unexplored territory together.

WHY HAVE BELIEFS? WHY NOT JUST HAVE RULES?

Teachers sometimes ask, "Why have beliefs? Why not just have rules? Rather than tell them the answer to this question, I like to have teachers discover the answer to this question. I ask them to think about a rule or a law they observe in the community. An example would be to follow the speed limit. Then I ask them why do we have a law about speed limits? Their common response is to be safe. Since I want them to feel the difference between a law and a belief at a visceral level I finally ask them, how do you feel when I say, "follow the speed limit" or "drive so you and others are safe." The other example I like to use is the law about "pay your taxes" or the belief to "support your community." Then I use a rule that teachers follow at school and give the supporting belief. For example, I ask them how do you feel when I say, "write your lesson plans" or "be prepared to teach your students or be prepared for a substitute teacher." It can be a personal rule such as "no smoking on the premises" which supports the belief, "model a healthy life style." After a few examples teachers usually feel why it is important to have beliefs. Beliefs are more internally motivating. People have more energy and enthusiasm for living by their beliefs rather than following rules. Students feel the same as teachers. Students need to hear more than just rules which tell them what not to do. For example, walk, don't run in the halls, don't wear hats, keep your hands and feet to yourself and don't chew gum are not very motivating. Students will have more interest and motivation if they hear belief statements. For example, together everyone achieves more, caring means sharing, respect yourself and others, be safe, together we can solve any problem.

Sometimes a teacher asks, "What do you do if students have different beliefs?" I like what Stephen Covey says, "The six major world religions all teach the same basic core beliefs...I find a universal belief in fairness, kindness, dignity, charity, integrity, honesty, quality, service, and patience."

He goes on to say that, "people may argue about how these principles are to be defined, interpreted, and applied in real-life situations, but they generally agree about their intrinsic merit. They may not live in total harmony with them, but they believe in them. And they want to be managed by them."[13]

I have worked in a dozen countries and in many socio-economic environments. When I ask the parents to list their family beliefs I never fail to be amazed at the similarities in what they say. When I was invited to the Jakarta International School in Indonesia we had two parent nights of over two hundred people each. It was heartening to hear how they fit the ideas of Restitution with their own cultures. For example, restoring a person by bringing up the strength from inside would be called "honor" in the Asian culture. In the Canadian aboriginal cultures the idea of restitution would be called "kwayeskitoti" in the prairies and "digitah" on the west coast. In Iceland the same concept is called "uppybbing." Below is an example of beliefs brainstormed by asking teachers to reflect on their family beliefs. Be sure when you do this that you first teach them to differentiate between the what (rule) and the why (belief behind the rule).

For example, in Southern Manitoba I was working with a group of 165 people in a school district. When we were developing our beliefs the custodian called out, "Don't fight over the inheritance." We had a good laugh, and then I asked him, "Why is that important?" He immediately responded, "Peace in the family" and we were at the belief level. If someone says, "Don't use violence" and we ask why, the answer will always be "Be safe." When doing this with students they frequently say something like, "Don't hog the ball" and when asked why the answer is "Be a team

---

[13] Stephen Covey, *The Seven Habits of Highly Effective People: Restoring the Character Ethic*, p.94-95

player." Then we ask, "Do you believe that?" Every time we address a belief we are strengthening our community and youth are reflecting on how they want to be. It is crucial that we are at the principle level when creating beliefs, this is the moral level. Say to youth, "We can't let you hurt what we have built to help each learn together. We want you to be a thinking person. Question everything. Do it with respect. Think about the kind of person you want to be and how you want to be treated. Think about whether you can be in harmony with us. Our group beliefs protect each individual. To the group each of us has an obligation for the safety and freedom we are guaranteed."

The following are examples of social contracts:

Team 231 - In this classroom, we believe...

- Respect others and their culture.
- Be responsible.
- You'll be safe if you have no weapons.
- Be a team, work together and give encouragement.
- Having fun is important.

Caterpillar Team List of Beliefs

- Maintain a positive attitude.
- Be an individual.
- Trust and respect others and their belongings.
- Commitment to projects and individual tastes.
- Help each other out.

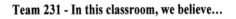

HOW TO ESTABLISH THE SOCIAL CONTRACT

Schools are creative about what they call the social contract and how they create it. The three most important words to remember about how to create the social contract are – process, process, process. The process is more important than the product. The social contract is not something the teacher writes and posts in the classroom. Together everyone is involved in creating a picture of how we want our classroom to be, how we want to treat each other, how we want to make decisions, how we want to resolve conflict, how we want to fix mistakes, and how we want our classroom to look, sound and feel.

RESPECT Y-CHART

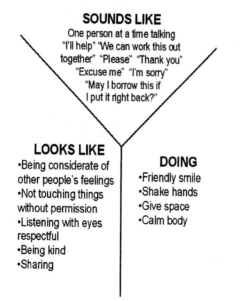

SOUNDS LIKE
One person at a time talking
"I'll help" "We can work this out
together" "Please" "Thank you"
"Excuse me" "I'm sorry"
"May I borrow this if
I put it right back?"

LOOKS LIKE
•Being considerate of
other people's feelings
•Not touching things
without permission
•Listening with eyes
respectful
•Being kind
•Sharing

DOING
•Friendly smile
•Shake hands
•Give space
•Calm body

There are many different ways to create the social contract. One variable to consider is the age of the students. Another consideration is the size of the group or how the school is organized. Primary teachers that meet with the same group of students all day usually create a classroom agreement with their class. Intermediate and middle school teachers can develop a classroom agreement with each class, or meet as a grade-level or team to create a team or grade-level agreement. High schools can use any process above or even create a school-wide belief statement. The important thing is that every person in the school has had a chance to think about it. It is also important to revisit the social contract on a regular basis and discuss beliefs in a content other than discipline.

When learning about Restitution and establishing the social contract it is helpful to understand that we have different levels of perception. William Powers[14], the founder of Perceptual Control Theory, has developed a hierarchy of eleven levels of perception which can be studied. For the purposes of Restitution, we have combined these into four clusters: what, why, who and how.

The Healing Cycle

WHO	*Person I Want To Be	System Concepts Level (identity)
WHY	*Universal Beliefs *Social Contract *Constitution	Principle Level (belief)
WHAT	*Rules and Roles *Expectations	Program Level (rote)
HOW	*T-charts and Plan	Sensory Level (concrete)

---

[14] William Powers, *Making Sense of Behavior: The Meaning of Control*, New Canaan, 1998.

The 'how' is the detailed plans. The 'what' represents the rules which become programmed automatically. The 'why' is the beliefs I hold, and the 'who' is the person I will be if I hold this belief.

When I used to go to schools as a discipline consultant teachers would ask me "**What** rules should we have?" and "**How** can we make kids follow them?" I would always ask "**Why** do you have these rules and **who** do you want to be in the life of these children?" By asking the staff these questions I was helping them bump up their perceptions of discipline from the concrete to the philosophical level where they could evaluate their practices to see if they were in line with their goals and their mission statement. Restitution focuses on the **why** and the **who** questions.

PITFALLS OF THE SOCIAL CONTRACT: MIXING BELIEFS AND RULES

When we brainstorm with children asking, "What kind of classroom do we want to have?" we must be careful to bump up their responses to the level of beliefs rather than expectations or rules. For example one class for their Social Contract had "Be kind, work hard, and keep our classroom clean." The first two components are beliefs because they are general, philosophical and speak to the ideal person. The third concept "Keep our classroom clean" is more concrete. It is a rule or procedure rather than a belief. For the teacher to move this statement to the belief level it is important to ask, "Why would we want to keep our classroom clean?" to search for the idea of "Respecting our environment."

Ruth Charney[15] whose work I respect gives the following examples of rules in *Teaching Children To Care*.

1. We will treat each other fair.
2. We will keep quiet when others are working.
3. We will help teachers or classmates when they ask for help.
4. We will walk in the halls and in the classroom.
5. We will try to solve disagreements by talking it over ourselves. If we can't, we will ask the teacher to help.
6. We will use only the things we need and put the tops back on stuff.

I would like to use this as a jumping off point because she does such a specific job of analyzing them. Numbers one, three and five are beliefs. Numbers two, four and six are rules. When Charney analyzes the belief statements she is aware of the differences. Number one she said resulted in many discussions about what was fair. We would say there was an opportunity to Y-chart this belief. Number three she termed effective and number five she said was, "a true ideal of passionate interest to children." How do we know numbers two, four and six are rules? Number two she said needed frequent reminders which shows it was a rule to be monitored. The belief behind it would be something like, "We believe in a learning environment for all." Number four was "clear cut and easy to monitor" and number six was "too narrow." We would say it was at the rote or program level of a rule.

We have many teachers who tell us they like to combine Responsive Classroom with Restitution. We can see why because our philosophies are so similar. However, teachers use Restitution to make the essential

---

[15] Ruth Charney, *Teaching Children To Care*, Greenfield: Northeast Foundation for Children, 1994. p. 60.

differentiation between rules and beliefs and to move beyond consequences to an internal focus. They use rules as a fall back position and they use weaving.

I was chagrined to read Robert Marzano's[16] book *Classroom Management That Works* only to find that in every program he reviewed the behavior management worked off rules and enormous amounts of time were spent on recording and on analyzing the problem. Restitution does not do this. We feel it is a waste of time to record multiple instances of pushing or swearing on a playground. Students do this because they don't know another way to be. Their behavior is purposeful. It meets a need for them. It is the best they know at the time. Telling them to stop meeting their need to instead meet ours doesn't work in the long term. Unless we move away from measuring and analyzing the misbehavior to helping students to learn their needs and to create new pictures for themselves of the persons they want to be, real change will not take place. Restitution has dozens of programs in their second decade where discipline has become a non-issue because the proactive work has been done. We cannot get self discipline from rules. We can only get temporary self control and compliance. We need to address beliefs to build internal strength and creative solution finding. Our challenge is to assess this growth.

In some schools I found much work had been done on the philosophy of education and learning. The staff wanted to help students become life long learners, caring members of their community and global citizens of an ever

---

[16] Robert Marzano, *Classroom Management That Works*, Alexandria: Association for Supervision and Curriculum Development, 2003.

changing world. These were lofty goals. When I asked them, "**Who** do you want to be?" and "**Why** is change important?" they knew the answers. However when I asked, "**What** programs or routines do you have to express your principles?" or "**How** exactly do you plan to help students become self directed learners?" they drew a blank. They did not have practices that were aligned with who they wanted to be or with their beliefs.

Where is your school strong? The **what** and the **how** are always clearly spelled out in behavior modification practices which believe in the external control of counting and measuring. The **who** and the **why** which are necessary to move to Restitution can be found in character education or expectations. All four, the **who**, **why**, **what**, and **how** must be processed in establishing the social contract.

Elementary Example

Below is an example of a process for establishing the social contract with primary students using all four levels: **who, why, what, and how.** The **what** represents rules. **Why** represents beliefs. **How** represents specifics as shown in a Y chart. **Who** stands for the person we want to be. Since they know rules we start there and bump up to beliefs.

What	1.	Elicit the **rules** (misbehavior descriptors).
What	2.	Shift the rules from **don't rules** to **do rules** (desired behavior descriptors). Most teachers have learned this.
Why	3.	To get beliefs ask the students, "**Why do** we have these rules? Why is it important? How is it better for you? For others?"

Why	4.	Ask, "What do we **believe** if we have these rules?" Create a list by clustering rules and bumping up to the beliefs.
How	5.	If I see something that might hurt, how exactly do you want me to be talking to you? Should I be saying, "What's the rule?" or do you want me to say, "What do we believe? Do you believe it?" What will I see or hear you doing?
Why	6.	Does your family believe in fairness, respect and kindness?
Who	7.	What kind of person will it help you be if you think about our beliefs? Have you got a picture of yourself?
How	8.	O.K., now let's see if our beliefs work. If we are being kind at the sand table, what would we see/hear? What would we be doing if someone wants into the group?
Why	9.	Tell me again, why are you going to do this? Do you think will it work?
Who	10.	Who will you be if you do it?

A Secondary Example

The following example was done in a middle school. The following was a dialogue with students.

> Pretend this is the best day in the best class in the world. What exactly would be happening? Think about it. What would you be seeing, hearing, and feeling when you walk into our class? In your small groups, I'd like you to create a Y-chart. Put your Y-charts on the wall and let's spend some time looking at them.

For some classes, you might want to structure it so that two people from each group present their Y-chart to the others. The next step in the process is to ask, "If this is what we want to be seeing, hearing, feeling, and doing, what does this say about what we believe?" (Principle Level) Discussion may be done in small groups or in the whole group and the result will be a list of beliefs derived from the sensory descriptors of practices. The final question to ask is, "If we hold these beliefs, who will we be as a group? (Identity Level) What do the above practices and beliefs say about us?" The whole group discusses the above question until they arrive at a sentence or two that describe who they are. This will then become their vision. An example from Superior, WI would be "Come for the education; stay for the adventure." Another from Richfield High School is "We respect ourselves, and others. Together we have responsibility to make this an educational environment." If someone says, "What happens if a person doesn't do what we say we believe?" the first answer is to say, "We'll all talk to him and listen to what he says he believes." If they say, "What if he doesn't want to believe what we believe?" our answer will be, "We can't make a person believe something so the teacher will just have to use rules if what he does is hurting others or our learning. We can't force a person to sign our social contract. People have the right to sit and think."

A PROCESS FOR STAFF BELIEFS [17]

Many times a faculty may want to establish a social contract to clarify their beliefs about how they want to treat each other. Here's a common process.

- Each writes down their own family beliefs. (2 minutes)
- Share beliefs in groups of 4-6 people. Seek to understand. (4-6 minutes)
- Come to consensus on beliefs the whole group agrees on. Write them down. (4 minutes)

---

[17] Dr. Judy Anderson, "The Social Contract" from *Building A Quality School*, Saskatoon: Chelsom Consultants Limited, 1996.

Restitution Schools Report

- Large group develops a belief list. (5-10 minutes)
- Clarify terms on list.
- Identify needs behind beliefs.
- Dialogue about a term where there is not agreement.
- Establish small groups to dialogue over the next few months.

This activity is also an excellent one to use with parent groups. It takes less than 30 minutes and inevitably parents ask for the list from other groups so they can go home and talk about them with their children

Other Pitfalls to Watch Out For

One school had been using work, respect and belong in their code of conduct. They wanted to keep those words. The words work, respect, and belong are actually beliefs and are not rules. They belong on the Restitution side. However, I have found that if these words were previously part of a consequence model they are tainted. They can't be transferred to a restorative model because the students out of habit will ask, "What happens if we don't work? respect? belong?" and we are back to sanctions. In Restitution it is key that the students create the belief words by discussing their family beliefs or by reflecting on the kind of person they want to be. There are many good character education programs such as the Virtues Program[18], but we must be careful. A character education list will be useful if it is first elicited from the students. The words are valuable but the process may be presented in a manner that is external not internal. For example if we say that this week we will study tolerance or ask students to grade themselves on kindness it will not help them look inside. However,

---

[18] Kavelin-Popov, Linda. *The Virtues Project Educator's Guide: Simple Ways to Create a Culture of Character.* Jalmar Press, 2000

once the students have created their list of beliefs the lessons are marvelous to use.

A working belief statement cannot be an exhaustive list. Start with two or three concepts and create something fun and zippy that we want to ask students to repeat. Putting a belief statement in the form of a rap or song with movement will help some students remember it and make it more fun. Jeff Grumley of the Restitution Peace Project outlines how to do this in *The Connected School*[19]. Check with www.realrestitution.com for examples.

HOW TO KEEP THE SOCIAL CONTRACT ALIVE

Creating the social contract is just the first step in the process. Deciding how to teach, to model, and to keep it alive are the next steps. Think of ways to keep the social contract visible. Teachers can display the classroom agreement in their room. Some teachers have students sign the agreement. Parent newsletters or parent handbooks are ways to share classroom agreements or school-wide belief statements with parents. Some schools have a belief wall near the office. The belief wall is a place where each classroom or grade-level displays their belief statements. Common beliefs (usually including respect, responsibility, safety, caring, honesty) are easily identified and those belief words can be posted on the wall above the classroom agreements. Children can sign their names on paper hands or leaves.

---

[19] E. Perry Good, Jeff Grumley, Shelley Roy, *A Connected School*, Chapel Hill: New View, 2003, p. 149.

Another way to keep the social contract visible is to print it on things. The parent association at Sheridan Hills Elementary gave all staff and students a T-shirt with the four core values - respect, responsibility, caring and honesty. Hastings Middle School gave students a wristband with the four needs (belonging, power, fun and freedom). A Richfield High School science teacher gave students a business card with the four needs on one side and the behavior components on the other side. Class meetings provide opportunities to revisit the classroom agreement to solve problems or self-evaluate how we are living our beliefs. A class can pick one of their beliefs to focus on for the next week. Student journaling is another way for each student to self-evaluate. These writings can be shared with parents.

SUMMARY OF BELIEFS

1. Beliefs are more abstract than rules which are specific and concrete.
2. Core beliefs are universal.
3. Group beliefs can be constructed through meaningful dialogue.
4. Beliefs must not be cumbersome or people can't remember them.
5. We can energize children's group beliefs through rhythm or song.
6. Beliefs are to be used to guide our decisions about relationships about learning and about democratic management.
7. Beliefs need to be revisited regularly to be a moving force.
8. When a belief changes it impacts many of our practices and this can happen quickly for better or for worse.
9. We, in a school, are partners with the parents in helping youth develop their beliefs.
10. We need to align what we want, what we know, and what we are actually doing with our beliefs to ascertain if we are being congruent.

BOTTOM LINES PROTECT BELIEFS

Some people when they hear "bottom line" think of punishment. This is not our meaning. The purpose of a bottom line is to preserve the social contract we all make together. We cannot let individuals override what the group decides though we welcome their questions, even their dissent to help us define our boundaries and our purpose. If people don't want to look at themselves, to reflect on values or to make amends we can't change them. However if we are in a position of responsibility and we are accountable we have to fall back to the external discipline of the monitor position. Particularly we need to protect people from being injured. For this we need bottom lines.

The bottom line is used when an individual is deemed to interfere with a belief the group holds dear. Usually the person who offends is sent away from the group. The removal could be from the classroom, playground, gym, lunchroom or the school depending on the severity of the threat posed to others. We try to use bottom lines sparingly and do so only when we have been unable to create conditions for the person to think and to manage themselves in a responsible, non-hurting way. A bottom line is a last resort and all staff must be involved in creating the bottom lines, having a common picture of what constitutes bottom lines and they need to show consistency on following through.

To help teachers get the bottom line I often ask, "What do parents say is totally unacceptable—they would not send their child to school if this is happening?" We find parents do not want to send their children to school where there is violence, drug use, harassment, or no learning. Students do not feel safe if the teacher cannot gain control of the class or playground in dangerous situations. Staff and parents need to decide which behaviors are totally unacceptable to us as "community." Bottom lines need to be agreed upon and consistently upheld publicly so students see we adults are serious about safety and learning. To be upheld publicly is not to have the child parade with a placard which says "I steal" or "I bite." It means the adult in the situation calmly stating, "This behavior is not acceptable, it is against what we believe."

First we list the bottom lines then we find the belief that rule protects.

Bottom Lines	Beliefs
• No Harassment	• Respect
• No Violence	• Safety
• No Drugs	• Health
• No Weapons	• Safety
• No Direct Defiance	• Learning

We Walk Our Talk

Many programs have suggested the establishment of zero tolerance for certain offences. The bottom lines in Restitution are zero tolerance yet they go much further. The first thing to understand about the bottom lines in Restitution is that they are established to protect the beliefs which the group holds dear because bottom lines reflect the will of the community and need to be established in conjunction with the parents and other community players. When a bottom line is broken and is addressed it needs to be clearly tied to the belief behind it. For example, if a racist comment is made in the lunch room a supervisor needs to say, "That is not okay to say (rule). In our school we believe in respect (belief). Come with me." and take the student out or if cheating occurs a coach might yell, "Stop! This can't happen (rule) then calmly say, "We believe in fair play. Go to the bench" or if drugs are discovered an administrator might say, "These are not legal (rule). We believe in a healthy life style in our school (belief). Has anyone talked to you about this?" If a teacher cannot teach her class due to a student's misbehavior and she has exhausted her resources, the principal should say, "Mrs. Clark would not have sent you out if it wasn't serious. Here we believe in learning."

When I was trained as a counselor I learned to take students aside to have conversations with them. This prevented their embarrassment and avoided giving them a stage in front of other students. With Restitution when a bottom line is violated publicly, for example a student visits sexual harassment upon another and it hurts our beliefs about respect and equality, that belief must be publicly restored, then we take the student away from the group. If the comment is left untied to the belief, the damage remains.

The second issue I would like to address with regard to bottom lines is that if used alone they will not suffice. They will act as a deterrent for a brief period especially if they are new to the student body. However, we need to use that time to educate the students in self discipline - to teach them to manage their emotions, to understand their own needs, manage their actions to think about who they want to be and to create common beliefs.

Restitution Schools Report

ADMINISTRATION AND THE BOTTOM LINE

One of the complaints I hear most often from teachers is that their administration is not clear about the bottom line. The bottom line is not solely the responsibility of administration. Establishing the bottom line will be a staff, community and, later on, a student responsibility. Once this is done, if the bottom line is not followed it is the job of administration to question staff and to firm up the bottom line. It is also the responsibility of the principal to clearly communicate the bottom line to the student body and to support teachers who find themselves in need of invoking it. When students are sent out of class by teachers to the principal, they need to indicate to the administrator that the situation is serious by saying a phrase such as, "Latitia doesn't seem to understand we're serious about safety." The removal must be termed a consequence. It is not a restitution. A restitution may take place later, but bottom line behaviors are serious enough to present the need for immediate removal from the group. If a child refuses to leave a class each school needs a back up plan. Usually an administrator or counselor comes to the door for the student and they leave.

Now you may be wondering why we are talking monitoring when we believe in restitution. The reason is that I have learned an important lesson from schools moving to Restitution. Students initially tend to perceive Restitution as weakness. This is because they are so used to being controlled by our supervision. It will be particularly obvious if a classroom has had an authoritarian teacher. Students who perceive there are no limits will test to find out where the line is.

Schools have taught us that we can avoid this phenomenon if we firm up the bottom line at the same time as we move to belief centered discipline through Restitution. Not all students are ready for Restitution. For those who don't want to self evaluate and fix their problems we still need consequences. We don't spend a lot of time on this, under two minutes. Bottom lines are clear inviolate, agreed upon consequences. They apply to staff, students and visiting parents. While a positive school climate is one's best defense against violence in a school, we leaders must not be found wanting when a student makes a challenge. To allow intimidation, harassment, drug use or wanton disruption of learning is a powerful statement that we do not believe what we say. Removing a hurt student safely and calmly, speaks of self-respect and school respect.

Bottom lines frequently violated are those in which the student's behavior creates an unsafe situation. In the classroom it can be where their behavior is such that no learning can take place until they are removed. I sometimes describe this as the "knot in the stomach" situation. A student has been directly defiant to the teacher or teaching assistant. There is dead silence in the room. Everyone is looking to see what will happen and the teacher has a knot in the stomach. At this point no learning will take place. Unfortunately the environment has moved from win-win to win-lose and the teacher has to win or the class doesn't feel safe.

From our experience it is not a good idea to do a bottom line intervention and then attempt a restitution in the same time frame. The main reason for this is that a bottom line is serious; it is our heaviest monitoring tool and a student will be apprehensive when we flag the offense. In this state they can't learn. Their brains are downshifted. We don't have to lecture them or demean them for this to happen. They need a time to calm down and to reflect for an hour or a day. A second reason not to try to do bottom lines and restitution in tandem is that if you counsel the student using restitution he or she will not be the same at the end of the session and you'll be reluctant to impose the necessary consequence which comes with the bottom line. Bottom lines are used sparingly. They usually come after the teacher has made several interventions with the student. In Restitution most discipline problems are solved at the classroom level.

When I think back on all the times in the classroom when I was tough without thinking about why I was doing it or taking time to impart that to a student I feel sick! Too often there was no learning, merely a display of authority based on my fear of losing control. This need not be the situation today. When the community has established beliefs and bottom lines together, when we stand shoulder to shoulder firm in our shared beliefs, we can have a feeling of deep power from within and this feeling will lead to compassion for the person in front of us. We can verbalize why we do what we do and we can feel noble, not mean, when we protect our beliefs with our bottom lines.

EXAMPLES OF BOTTOM LINES

It is essential that the whole staff dialogue about where exactly the bottom lines should be and what belief is behind each one. Their decision is dependent on the norms of the community. For example there is a school in a Mennonite community that was able to establish "no swearing" as a bottom line. This was because the students didn't hear swearing at home or in the community. They would gasp if they heard it in the classroom. In most schools if students swear inadvertently (e.g. when they drop a book) and correct themselves it is not a bottom line but a situation for redirection to use appropriate language. All the schools I have worked with consider direct swearing at an adult in the school to be a bottom line on which to be acted. Our long term goal is always to be gradually setting the bottom line higher as students learn self discipline. Also this happens when they have less frustration to express. Another example, which is always a bottom line, is a threat to kill someone. For example, in one school in which I worked a student said to a teacher, "If I don't pass this class someone's going to get killed." The teacher asked, "Do you mean to say that?" When the student repeated the statement with anger he was sent to the principal.

In another example a student in New York State wrote a note that threatened to kill a teacher and her child. I asked what the consequence had been. When the teacher said nothing happened, I told her that the bottom lines in her school were not strong enough. She replied that in New York legislation protecting special education students does not let schools suspend them. I believe that if this is the case the legislation needs to be reviewed. Schools need to be safe and that takes clout. I have not been at a high school that has not had to call in the police sometime during the year.

I have seen a third grade student carried kicking down the hall after he has stripped the rubber base board off the time out room. We had to call his mother to come and get him. We explained to her that we weren't equipped to handle his level of destruction. A similar conversation was had with another parent when a child kept running out of the school and we couldn't be responsible for her safety. A primary child who was crawling under the table biting other students' legs was dealt with as bottom line because the teacher couldn't teach. A student defecating on the floor in the washroom was a bottom line. It was confronted. He was sanctioned, and then we worked with him to manage his anger and help him be part of our group. Yelling "f... you" to a teacher is a bottom line. It violates respect. Throwing a plate down on the cafeteria line saying loudly, "This is slop" is a bottom line. However, if he had muttered while taking his plate with him it would not be a bottom line. We could have calmly said to him, "Then don't eat." It was a chance for redirection but not a bottom line as was the first example.

Aggravating Students

I say in workshops that any teacher has the power to aggravate a student into breaking a bottom line. The most common example is when a student refuses to do their work. This is not a bottom line situation if the student just sits. The teacher can say to him, "I'll get with you when I can," and move on to teach the class. If the teacher decides to force the student to work by standing over him and demanding compliance the bottom line can arrive quite quickly. In this case the staff is not practicing giving the student time to reflect. However, if this has been done and the student makes it impossible for the teacher to teach it is a bottom line because we believe in learning.

All school staff need to have an agreed upon picture of where the bottom line is. T-charts need to be done on violence, defiance, harassment, weapons and drugs. Then examples from teachers' experiences need to be run through the model to see if it is adequate to serve us. There is generally a common view of what are deemed serious incidents. If all staff, not just teachers, agree to uphold the staff bottom lines and administration agree to solidly back staff then you are on your way. Remember bottom lines are not just for students. They also govern our interactions with each other and our treatment of students and parents. Taking time to do bottom lines is putting strength in our beliefs. It gives us consistency on the most important of issues and predictability builds security and trust. Healthy relationships have bottom lines because bottom lines protect our common beliefs. The booklet, *Looks Like Sounds Like* gives many examples of bottom line T-charts created by students. These can't just be handed to your class because creating them together is a process.

Defiance

Looks Like/ Sounds Like	Does Not Look Like/ Sound Like
• Refusal to follow directions (e.g. "No, I won't!") • Profanity directed at an adult • Destructive behavior • Posing a danger to self or others • Making a personal threat (psychological, verbal, physical)	• Rolling eyes • Body language (talk) • Signs and mumbles • Sarcasm • Swearing (in general, not directed) • Stalling or procrastinating

A bottom line in Restitution is not viewed as a big hammer. A bottom line is put in place to separate an offending person from the group. We say, "Because you don't believe what we believe, let's use this space and time for you to reflect on our beliefs and to talk with us about yours. You can't change something if you don't understand. If we haven't explained to you why these things are important to us that is our part of the problem. We can't force you to believe and to honor what we have decided. Also, we can't let you hurt what we have built to help each learn together. We want you to be a thinking person. Question everything. Do it with respect. Think about the kind of person you want to be and how you want to be treated. Think about whether you can be in harmony with us. Our group beliefs protect each individual. To the group each of us has an obligation for the safety and freedom we are guaranteed."

FROM OLD THINK TO NEW THINK

Reflections from the Lake Country

Recently I worked with a middle school that had just started Restitution. From them I learned that we need to be more specific about how to make the transition from a consequence based discipline system to a system focused on building self discipline in the students. They were opening a new school and students were coming in from a number of elementary schools. The teachers were keen on moving to belief centered Restitution. However, these students who had been accustomed to consequences were dependent on adults for the setting of rules. When the rules were suddenly not there the students perceived they had license to do what ever they wanted. They thought "There are no limits here." Students who have not been taught to look inside and self evaluate are looking to us to have to a privilege removed or a consequence invoked. When this does not happen they start to test to find out what they can get away with.

This was exhausting for the teachers who found themselves working harder than the youth. They got tired of having multiple conversations over petty issues such as not bringing supplies or being late. They were not restorative conversations. There was no self reflection. These were paybacks and were not strengthening for the youth; they found no genuine desire for reparation of the situation. This was particularly true because the teachers used a discipline form that resembled an old consequences plan form.

Old Think

It is common for a discipline form to ask for a statement of the problem and to ask the student to identify how what they did impacted others. The student then is asked to make a plan. The plan is usually to say "I'm sorry" and to desist from the identified misbehavior. We have all used these forms and students recognize them. They think completing the form is the solution. They believe when they fill it in that they are actually capable of stopping what they are doing. They do it, for awhile. For long term change, learning and meeting their needs is essential.

New Think

In Restitution we seldom use a form because our focus is on the conversation. If we use the Restitution Re-Thinking Sheet it is to help the student to think things through. The first question we ask to calm the student down is, "Is it okay to make a mistake? This is one of our beliefs because mistakes are how we learn." We then ask about the need the youth was attempting to meet by the problem behavior. We say, "What was it getting you? Belonging? Power? Freedom? Fun? Safety?" This question is to help the youth understand their own motivation.

RESTITUTION RE-THINKING SHEET [20]

1. What do we believe? Is it okay to make a mistake? Yes [] No []

2. If yes was your answer, what was your mistake?

   _____

3. Is it okay to make a mistake? Yes [] No []

4. Could you have done worse? Yes [] No []

5. If yes, what would be worse?_____

6. So did you do the worst thing? Yes [] No []

7. In a way it was not a mistake. It helped you. Say how it helped you meet your need. (Love, Power, Freedom, Fun, Survival)

   _____

8. Can you think of a way to help yourself without hurting someone else. Think hard. It isn't easy. What can you do?_____

9. Do you want our help? Yes [] No [] If "yes", who?_____

10. What is your plan? How? When? Where?

11. How will it meet your need? _____

12. How will this get you stronger? _____

13. Is this what you want? [] Yes [] No

We next validate the need being met. "We understand it's important to stick up for yourself" or "We know friends are important." This is not condoning the misbehavior. The process of validating needs helps us to go "shoulder to shoulder" with the student. We view the problem as a solution to be found by asking, "How can you get what you need without hurting anyone else's need?" We know the answer has to be created so we give the student space to think. We don't accept, "I won't do it again" or "I'm sorry." We move to inventing a plan that strengthens the youth and helps the group.

When a student is stuck we ask if they have seen another person, a family member or a friend solve a similar problem. If they say "yes" we direct them to talk to that person and come back and tell us what they learned. If they say "no" we ask if they want a suggestion from us. We give several so they need to evaluate them rather than grasping one.

Planning Circles

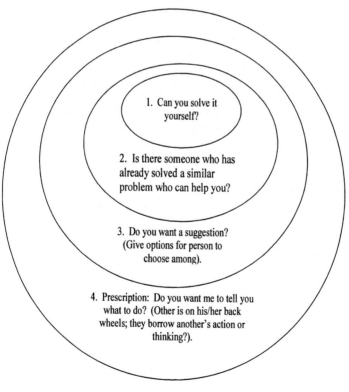

1. Can you solve it yourself?

2. Is there someone who has already solved a similar problem who can help you?

3. Do you want a suggestion? (Give options for person to choose among).

4. Prescription: Do you want me to tell you what to do? (Other is on his/her back wheels; they borrow another's action or thinking?).

---

[20] Restitution I Curriculum, Saskatoon: Chelsom Consultants Limited.

Sometimes we have no ready answers. When this happens we ask the student "Do you think it's going to be easy to figure this out?" When they respond "no" we agree with them and ask, "Do you want to work together to try and think up a solution?" We say, "You think about it and I'll think about it and maybe we can create a better way so both parties can get what they need. There are no simple answers to complex questions." When we and the student invent a plan we know we are in the right arena if there is high energy and if the student is excited to try it. We close the session with the question, "How will it be better for you if you do this? Don't answer me answer yourself." When a plan is created this way they are always excited to report their success to us.

SUMMARY OF BOTTOM LINES

1. Bottom lines **protect our beliefs**. They can not exist in a vacuum.

2. Bottom lines create **consistency** of purpose among all members.

3. Bottom lines express the power of the **group will**.

4. **Healthy relationships** have bottom lines.

5. Bottom lines show **we care**.

6. Bottom lines define where we will spend our time and where **we stop working harder** than the person we're trying to help. They conserve our energy.

7. Bottom lines display courage and **strength** of commitment.

8. Bottom lines keep **safety** in the group.

APPRECIATION TO RESTITUTION SCHOOLS

The process of Restitution is one which involves systemic change. What is this change? It is a change from boss manager to a transformational leader. To move into transformational leadership it is necessary to create a group vision and to practice share decision making. This happens in the classroom and in the school and it also needs support at the district level.

In each of the sites you will be reading about in the appendix there were decisions being made to share power between leaders and those who were led. In a school this means the principal shares information with staff and involves them in deciding about how we can best work with students. In the community it means informing parents, inviting them to participate in training events and having their children teach them what they are learning about human needs and how they have developed their class social contract.

When parents see the students in leadership roles they become more confident of the youths' capacity to be self directed learners. When students self evaluate that they have made a mistake and share with their parents how they have fixed it, parents are surprised and pleased at the strength and responsibility the youth are developing. Even small children can learn to manage themselves and to ask for what they need. One parent at a meeting said to me. "Now I understand what my five year old is learning." This week she said to me, "Mommy, your power is hurting my freedom. We have to help each other."

I have been working with over two hundred schools in the Twin Cities of Minneapolis and St. Paul. After the first few years of working with elementary schools, the middle school administrators started to attend Restitution trainings. They said, "We can't treat these students coming up from the elementary school the same way once they've had Restitution. They ask many questions and they want us to help them find solutions. We can tell the schools that are using Restitution."

In the families when parents practice self restitution they will find their children follow suit. They also will accept that the family has to have bottom lines to protect the important beliefs all hold. In the classroom students show more ability to deal with curriculum that requires them to be independent thinkers. They also have more skills to use in cooperative learning activities. It seems that they are finally ready to engage in more constructivist learning by being partners with the teacher in planning how best to approach the task so all can successful. When this energy is harnessed, learning becomes fun and grade scores go up.

Students are also taking responsibility for solving problems among themselves in a peaceful way. For example in Richfield High School administrators were told that a gang of youth would be gathering after school. When they asked students what assistance they wanted they were told "You don't have to do anything. All we want you to do is help us figure it out for ourselves." On another occasion when there seemed to be some cultural misunderstandings, the students created a solution by supporting a Hispanic dance event. At Roseville High School a school of 2000 students, when all grade nine students learned about their needs through literature, the administrators noticed they could solve referrals much more quickly. Students are also using the Restitution relationship principles to create stronger friendships with educators and to solve problems.

Restitution is a self discipline initiative which owes much to Canadian Aboriginal relationship practices. It also has roots in self control theory practices. There is a strong emphasis on personal freedom in the Restitution model. However, this is balanced by the desire to cooperate and to contribute to the greater good. As we look out at the global strife we can see people struggling to attain a balance between independence and group harmony. We can see different ethnic populations struggling to maintain their identity while needing to cooperate as part of a greater economic whole. The old discipline models of "Do it or I'll hurt you" or those which bribe people are eroding the human moral values we all hold. I hope the practices of Restitution will give our youth an alternative way to negotiate at many levels. What do we all believe? What is our common ground? How can we create structures so all can get what they need? Who will we be if we can do this?

When I look over our list of resources and reflect on all the books therein that have come out just since 2000 it is awe inspiring. The 21st century has brought with it a new way of thinking about relationships and systems. I am laughing as I write this because what I am realizing is this new way is also an old way of thinking. When we lived in communities with the same people for many years and could not jet away and relocate, we had to solve problems. We did not rely on sound bites but sought to understand. We knew the importance of honoring differences, of saving face, and of creating win-win long term solutions. The older wiser societies focused not on respect due to position, but on a deeper respect, that due a human being. Restitution Self Discipline recaptures for us a kinder more helpful way we can be with each other. I hope the stories you have read have given you information and some hope that we can teach our budding global citizens to live in harmony and in joy.

I am grateful for the ideas of Restitution I have learned from my teachers. I am thankful for the support of elders who have risen to speak in public meetings to support the direction of healing. I know you will be amazed at the creativity of the Restitution facilitators, trainers and teachers in how they have invented Restitution in their own way with their communities. To practise restorative restitution it is necessary to have an abundance mentality, to believe we can create a goal and then we can find the resources to make our dream for children happen.

It is a joy to walk through a school where the teachers have worked with the children to create real community. The school is full of energy. Children are solving their own problems. They are kind to each other and inclusive. They are excited to show us their belief statements on the walls of the school. They are not afraid to question what they are being taught. They laugh a lot and use this as an impetuous to invent new ways of being together. Please join us in this journey.

APPENDIX

RESTITUTION SCHOOLS REPORT

This section contains reports from schools and districts on their work with Restitution. Some of them are concise, others contain personal reflections. Over the past decade there have been Restitution trainings in over a thousand schools. These submissions are chosen to illustrate the diversity of programs. They range from a school of 250 to a district of 25,000 students.

ELEMENTARY SCHOOLS

Princess Alexandra Community School, Saskatoon, Sk

Princess Alexandra Community School in Saskatoon, Saskatchewan, is an inner city town school. It is half a block from the railroad tracks and shares a parking lot with a bingo hall. Princess Alexandra has an enrollment of 250–300 students from kindergarten to grade eight, 98% of them are aboriginal. It is a community school. Most children walk to school. In 1999 the Saskatoon School Board did a study and found to it's surprise that in the previous decade not one student who had graduated from grade eight from Princess Alexandra had gone on to graduate from high school. In the past four years the board decided to support Restitution training and dramatic changes are taking place. The school has gone from thirty seven incidents of discipline a day to two per day. 55% of the students are now at the median scores of the Canadian Test of Basic Skills whereas three years ago it was 7%. In the third year each student who left grade one could read.

90% of the parents in the community are involved with the school. Princess Alexandra received a $15,000 grant from the Saskatchewan Teacher's Federation to study the relationship between Restitution Self Discipline and aboriginal child rearing practices. Princess Alexandra has been recognized as one of ten outstanding aboriginal schools in Canada in 2003. It was the only urban school to be so honored. Yves Bousquet and Ted Amendt have spearheaded this program. Elders Katy Poundmaker, Ina Ahenakew and Edward Baldhead have provided guidance. The Princess Alexandra staff has given Restitution many ideas.

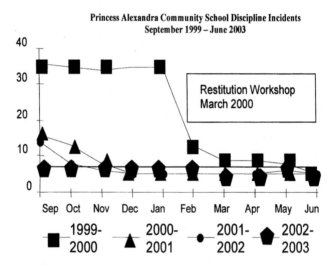

Princess Alexandra Community School Discipline Incidents
September 1999 – June 2003

Restitution Workshop March 2000

1999-2000   2000-2001   2001-2002   2002-2003

Princess Alexandra Community School Update

- In 1998, only 7% of our students in grade 4 performed at the 50th percentile on the Canadian Achievement Test (CAT).

- In 2000, 40% of our students in grade 4 performed at the 50th percentile on the Canadian Achievement Test (CAT).

Restitution Schools Report

- In 2002, 55% of our grade 4 students are at or above the 50% percentile on the Canadian Achievement Test (CAT).
- In 2004 each student who left Grade 1 could read.

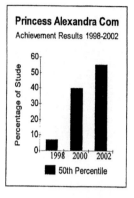

Princess Alexandra Com
Achievement Results 1998-2002

Submitted by Yves Bousquet, Principal

Reindeer Lake School – Southend, Saskatchewan[21]

Reindeer Lake School is located in Southend, which lies at the southern end of Reindeer Lake, about 8000 kilometers north of U.S. border. The school serves about 400 students from nursery school to Grade 12, including a day-care and a Head Start program as well as number of adults taking high school programs. There are 52 full time workers in the school. The school operates under the direction of a local education committee of the Peter Ballantyne Cree Nation Band council.

The inclusion of elders and cultural advisors is also significant as part of the leadership structure at Reindeer Lake School. While it could be said that the education committee were a group of elders, committee members actually

---

[21] David Bell, *Sharing Our Success: Ten Case Studies in Aboriginal Schooling*, Society for the Advancement of Excellence in Education, 2004, p.249-272

pointed to others in the community as elders and their unique source of influence on student success. An example provided was that the elders often confronted students they saw out in the community during schools hours as to why they were not in school. Elders were respected and this sort of intervention was suggested as impacting better attendance on the part of students.

The Restitution program instituted at Reindeer Lake in the 2002/2003 academic year has proven very successful. In 2001/2002 there were 371 suspensions from school. In the year following the adoption of the restitution approach, suspensions were reduced to 99. The number of "out of school" suspensions for the last three Septembers shows a marked decline. It is anticipated that this annual suspension rate will be reduced even further in 2004. This trend is a powerful indicator of an improving school climate that is a direct result of the active intervention of the school and the programs used to correct this problem.

Reindeer Lake School Number of Suspensions

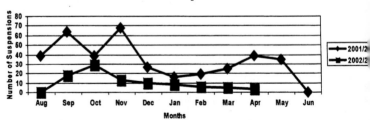

Totals:	Staff Training:
Aug 2001-Mar 2002 = 262 (Year - 336)	Restitution I –August 2002
Aug 2002-Mar 2003 = 89 (decrease of 66%)	Restitution II –March 2003

Bismarck School District, Bismarck, ND

Bismarck School District has been involved in Restitution since 1996. The first school to try Restitution was Jeannette Myhre Elementary School led by principal Bill Demaree. It is situated in downtown Bismarck next to the mall and the trailer court. They have trained all their staff in Restitution, even their volunteer grandparents. The first thing a person sees when they come into the school is the Circle of Life which holds ribbons with each child's name on them. This is their commitment to their beliefs. Fran Rodenberg, who has been principal of three elementary schools, Roosevelt, Pioneer and Riverside, has worked creatively to combine Restitution, Asset Building, and Integrated Thematic Instruction to build success for students. The ideas of Restitution have received great support from the district's superintendent, Paul Johnson.

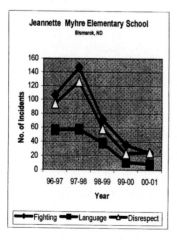

Kindergarten to Grade 6, Average 410-430 students, Urban school with high poverty - 55%.

Submitted by Bill Demaree

MIDDLE SCHOOLS

Central Middle School, Eden Prairie, Minnesota

With 1800 students, Eden Prairie is the second largest middle school in Minnesota. We are located in a suburb of the twin cities. Several of the elementary schools in Eden Prairie which feed into Central Middle School are using Restitution so the students come to the school oriented to self discipline. Many staff in the district as well as parents have had training in Restitution.

District Student Management Philosophy

We believe...

- Students, staff, parents, and community will design, communicate and participate as a partnership of self-motivated learners who assume responsibility for their personal actions.
- Problem-solving strategies taught in a positive and supportive environment foster the development of personal and mutual respect. These include strategies such as goal setting, peer mediation, conflict resolution, restitution and self evaluation.
- Promoting a sense of belonging focused on the learners' individual needs provides a safe and respectful environment.

Central Middle School Student Management Mission Statement

The mission of Student Management of CMS is for all staff members to interact with students in a manner that promotes responsible, respectful and self-directed behavior. Central Middle School will foster a partnership with students, staff and parents to establish clear expectations for respect of self, others and school in order to create a safe, secure environment in which everyone can learn.

Program Description

The student management program at CMS is comprised of three arenas of delivery: classrooms/teams, the planning room, and the office. The philosophy of Control Theory and Restitution underlines the student management efforts at CMS. We believe that all behavior is intentional in order to meet a need. We believe in providing a need-fulfilling environment and in encouraging students to be self-responsible and internally motivated. In accordance with these beliefs, we aim to use the least coercive discipline possible for each situation.

The majority of student management at CMS occurs within the classrooms of the specific teams. At the beginning of the year, each team develops a covenant with their students which addresses student and teacher needs and expectations. When inappropriate behavior occurs in the classroom, this covenant then becomes a reference point of teacher-student discussions. Through these conversations, teachers and students develop a plan for future behavior.

Teachers on each team meet on a regular basis to discuss student management issues that are occurring in their classrooms. This approach allows for the development of successful interventions that address the team needs of the students and the teachers. This philosophy of team-based student management is consistent with our overall philosophy of respect and responsibility. Each team is assigned a Dean of Students to help in this process as needed. Because the school is so large there is a restitution staff member who wears a beeper. She can be summoned to any room to assist a student with his/her behavior or to relieve a staff member to talk with a student. She escorts students who need thinking time to the planning room.

The planning room is a learning place where students can process their behavior, and devise a plan for improvement or restitution. The students are assisted in developing a plan to understand and control their behavior. The planning room supervisor works with the students helping them work through their self evaluation and planning. The plan created becomes an opportunity for students to restore themselves for re-entry to the student population. The supervisor helps students share that information with the affected teachers and others. Teachers communicate with the supervisor about the expectations for planning, and possible consequences if the student is not willing to plan. The planning room is an integral part of teaching restitution to students.

When a team of the planning room has been unable to successfully intervene in a student management issue, or if the issue involves one of the school's bottom line behaviors, the issue is referred to the Student Management Office. Hallway and bus issues are also addressed in the office. The Student management office works with the individual to:

1) Take responsibility for the behavior.

2) Understand the reasons behind the behavior.

3) Develop an alternative means for meeting the needs behind the behavior

4) Create a plan to restore any damage created by the behavior.

At CMS, we have clear bottom lines: fighting/physical intimidation, harassment, serious insubordination, possession/use of weapon, and possession/use of chemicals. These bottom lines represent those behaviors which will not be tolerated at CMS.

The teachers at CMS have the choice of sending the student with a discipline issue to the Dean of Students for a consequence or sending the student to the planning room to work on a restitution plan. The first year 50% of the teachers chose to send the student to the Dean of Student for a consequence and 50% to the planning room. The second year, 20% of students were sent to the Dean of Students and 80% to the planning room. The third year 100% of students were sent to the planning room.

Restorative Suspension Pilot Program For Frequent Flyers

The goal of the restorative suspension program at Central Middle School is to create the conditions for students to fix their mistakes, change their behavior, and return to school strengthened, while spending productive time contributing service to the community.

The original pilot program involved the six students out of 1800 with the most suspensions. There are four parts to this program:

1. The student does community service at local senior home, bus barns, or kindergarten class therefore helping the community, instead of always being helped.
2. The student works with a tutor to catch up with academic work.
3. The student meets with a Restitution Planner.
4. The student meets with the person hurt to restore the relationship.

In the first semester there were 39 suspensions for a total of 112 days. In the second semester there were fourteen suspensions. In the in-take meeting the student meets with an administrator/dean and parent(s) after an incident occurs if the student is considered a suitable candidate. Restorative suspension may be assigned and must be agreed upon by a parent. The assignment length is determined by the administrator/dean (but not less than one day) and set up by the discipline clerk and a parent. Students who are considered violent are not welcome.

The student is transported to Prairie Adult Care by his/her parent or Dial-A-Ride (set up by parent) and brings his /her lunch. The student spends the day participating in community service with the senior citizens to show how they want to be part of their larger community. When the student returns to school, he/she will develop a restitution plan to strengthen the student and restore relationships, facilitated by a staff member trained in restitution planning. The student works with someone to catch up academically.

Re-entry meeting

This component is required before the student returns to classes. The meeting could include the student, other students, staff, teachers, from the student's team. The format could include a conflict mediation session, a small group meeting with the student and one or two others, or a large group meeting with a team. The emphasis is always on strengthening the student and restoring harmony in the group.

Prepared by CMS Staff and Sally Peterjohn, Restitution Trainer

Hastings Middle School, Hastings, Minnesota

Restitution Is A Lot Like Farming

The slow, steady process of implementing this type of a system-wide cultural paradigm shift is a lot like farming. There is an ebb and flow to the process like the seasons on the farm. Success is the sun that can encourage further growth or burnout even the most vigorous professional. Collegial support is the water that sustains life or by its absence allows the process to die on the vine.

Hastings is a bedroom community and suburb of St. Paul and Minneapolis, Minnesota. Hastings Middle School serves sixth, seventh, and eighth grade and uses a programming model that is a highbred between a traditional Junior High and more student-centered Middle School models. We are in the fifth year of implementing Restitution. There are 1320 students, 65 certified staff, 20 non-certified staff, and a three person administrative team.

One unique factor to our implementation plan that sets us apart from most other large schools is that we decided early on not to have a "planning room." The rationale behind this decision was based on feedback collected while doing site visits and interviews with schools that were three to five years ahead of us in implementation. We found that they were often struggling with an over-reliance on the planning room model. Lead staff in the buildings informed us that they believed that the planning room model allowed some teachers the chance to "send the problem away and wait for it to come back fixed." It also seemed counter-productive. Knowing that restitution needed to happen between the victims and offenders in an infraction we felt that the act of "making it right" should occur within the setting where the infraction occurred. We believed that this would help to build and maintain relationships between students and adults as well as increase the ownership of each solution that is developed.

As we continue to work toward a broader implementation of Restitution, three core findings continue to surface. (1) All stakeholders need to be aware of the direction of change, and those immediately responsible for the implementation need to deeply understand and believe in the process. (2) You need to say the right thing. The language is important. (3) You need to say the right thing correctly using the proper tone, body language, and facial expressions. It takes continued coaching, practise, reminding, and self evaluation because the difference between doing Restitution well and not doing it well is subtle and discrete.

Informing Stakeholders, Building Knowledge and Getting a Buy-in
During the year prior to the first year of implementation at Hastings Middle School we began the process of "opening up the territory." We sent formal and informal leaders on our staff to Restitution I training. They consistently returned enthusiastic to implement their newly learned information. We also worked on the building-level vision, mission statement and common beliefs. During our first year, we began slowly by using Restitution in several classrooms and sometimes in the office. We quickly realized the need to bolster our internal support capacity. In the second year, we were able to secure a grant that allowed for a significant amount of training and materials. Five staff members completed training in Restitution I, II, and III as well as a weeklong session in Control Theory. 60 % of our staff participated in

Restitution I training and 30% completed Restitution II. The summer between the second and third year we arranged an on-site training that resulted in two important factors. The critical mass of our building staff was trained in Restitution I and II, and we were able to introduce the concepts to staff from other buildings throughout the district.

In year four, we continued to build our internal capacity to get ourselves "unstuck." We had 20 staff members participate in Control Theory training, and we continued to keep the school board and district administration informed of our efforts. A significant challenge arose because of three years of dramatic budget reductions and staffing cuts. It is a huge challenge to maintain the "abundance mentality" when resources are in tight supply and there is not enough to go around. The challenge becomes avoiding competition for limited resources, at the same time that resources are depleted. We found that using consensus decision-making, and augmenting our budget through successful grant writing, helped greatly to maintain the spirit of cooperation. A group of interested staff members continued to meet to discuss the continued implementation of Restitution. We believed that our greatest challenges resulted from not having a concerted school-wide effort in teaching students the basic concepts of Restitution. We needed a vehicle to deliver the content.

During the fifth year, we began a homeroom period that met once a week and periodically introduced the key knowledge to students. As I reflect on where we are and how long it has taken us to get this far, there is one major hypothesis that I had that has been tested several times and almost every time it has been proven wrong. I understood that for teachers who taught under the reward and consequence paradigm, it would take a major intervention to complete the paradigm shift to a self-control, internal motivation paradigm. In fact, I believed that the longer a teacher had taught under the reward and consequence paradigm the longer it would take to complete the paradigm shift. Following this logic, I further hypothesized that if a newly licensed teacher began their career in a Control Theory and Restitution environment, they would not require any formal training to understand the concepts. I thought that they would learn from observing their peers interact with children in a non-coercive and non-punishing way they would pick it up. This hypothesis was wrong. Even for a new teacher, it takes a full two-day training experience to complete the conversion. This is strong evidence that the way we were educated and raised has a tremendous affect on us. A new teacher must overcome not only the behavior management they learn in the teacher preparation courses, but they must also overcome the more than 15 years role modeling they received as a students in the classrooms of punishers, buddies, and guilters.

You Need to Say the Right Thing

Language is very important. In order to assist us in the paradigm shift we produced banners, posters, logos on clothing, bracelets, tattoos, and countless cheat sheets to infuse the language of restitution into our environment. It is difficult to think of the right thing to say when you are working so hard to control your non-verbal communication. We developed laminated cheat sheets with important information on them so that teachers could keep the language handy. Many teachers taped the sheets to the wall so that they had a list of brief interventions they could use in front of them while they were teaching. We produced posters with large enough print that the teacher could see the general principals of Restitution from across the room. We encouraged teachers to hang the poster for their benefit in the back of the room so that they could refer to the poster while working with a child in conflict. We have essentially advertised the language of Restitution throughout our school. Questions are more important than statements. The perpetrators of a harm must arrive at their own way to fix it. The solution they create must be their own. The three most helpful hints I have found are: Focus on helping the offender get to the point where they forgive themselves as early as possible. They must believe that "it is okay to make a mistake" before they will be emotionally healthy enough to creatively find a way to fix it. Secondly, use wait time far more often, and for greater amounts of time than you ever imagined would be necessary. Often children may take more than a day to create a solution. Thirdly, if you cannot think of what to say, ask them what they would want a friend to do if they were in their shoes. This empathy-inspiring tactic works well even when the two kids involved in a conflict dislike each other.

You Need to Say the Right Thing Correctly

The non-verbal communication is as important as the words that are used. We often work in teams of two. This allows the primary speaker to carry on the bulk of the restorative conference while the secondary speaker can interject key questions or prompts, as well as to provide an observation for peer evaluation. After the child has left the conference, the primary person asks for feedback. Again, much of the evaluation comes in the form of questions rather than comments. Such as: "why did you decide to pursue the belonging need, after it seemed that the fun need was discovered?" Or, "do you think that the student will be able to follow-through on the plan they developed?" This helps the primary speaker to find their own style rather than mimicking that of the observer. I have been blessed with great colleagues. The staff at Hastings Middle School are capable, resilient, strong, caring, and creative. There is a saying that goes, "If you bloom where you were planted, be thankful for your roots." I have been fortunate to bloom where I was planted. I was a student and a teacher in the school where I am now the principal. I am deeply aware that this is why I so strongly believe in Restitution. They have forgiven me the transgressions of past, teaching me that it is okay to make a mistake. They have helped me to understand that each of us is so valuable that we must make every effort to make every one of us strong. By their role modeling they taught me as a child that the only discipline with staying power is self discipline. I thank them all for the influence my teachers have had on me in the past, the interdependent influence we have on each other today, and the influence that I have been empowered to have with others today and tomorrow. I am also grateful for the introduction to Restorative Justice and Restitution I received as an assistant principal in the South Saint Paul School District which adopted the ideas in 1998.

The biggest difference I have observed in my life as a result of Restitution is observed at the end of the day. I feel better at the end of the workday if I have helped kids solve problems and fix their mistakes, rather than if I have consequenced kids all day. When I get home to my wife and kids, I not only feel better than I would after a day of doling out consequences, but I also have a new skill set that allows me to be a more loving and capable spouse and father.

Submitted by Mark Zuzek - Principal

HIGH SCHOOLS

Roosevelt High School, Minneapolis, MN

Roosevelt is a downtown Minneapolis High School of 1500 students with a very ethnically mixed population.

Starting in school year 2000/2001 staff had Restitution and Control Theory training. At least one third of our teaching staff have had at least Restitution I and a number have had several trainings as well as Control Theory. Deans who deal with suspensions have especially been trained. We also use peer mediators some of whom have been trained. We have a student group called Unity that actively tries to stop negativity and supports positive peace efforts. We have a program called Reflect and Repair (R & R) that gives students various work activities to do if they have created problems in the building. We give Saturday school for infractions that might have generated suspensions previously. We also have administrators with more focus on hallway activity than we have had last year. Saturday School and R & R are "monitor" tools we use as we continue to suspend for bottom lines. We think all things are helping increase positives and decrease negatives in the building. The ideas of Restitution and Control Theory have been a great help as have been the specific practise we have learned for implementing these ideas.

You can see over three years that the fighting decreased quite dramatically as did this year's suspension rate. Here is our accounting of the decreases.

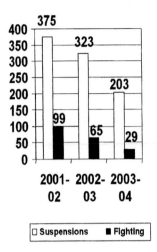

Submitted by Pat Palan

Assistant Principal & Restitution Facilitator

Below is a story from Roosevelt of teachers and parents pulling together to help create a peaceful environment.

In the autumn of 2001 a youth stabbed a fellow student. He was immediately suspended because use of violence is a bottom line. Our deans talked about how restitution could be used in this case. We talked about the option of the student reapplying the next year if he had sufficient counseling. However we knew a real restitution would involve looking at the underlying structure.

An examination of all the factors revealed where the conflict lay. Our school has a large population of Somali students and there was frequent friction between them and the African American population. It was such an encounter that had led to the stabbing. As we discussed possible restitutions we looked for common ground to create the good will to solve disputes.

Common ground was:

1.)   Both groups were black in America.

2.)   Both groups had historical roots in Africa.

3.)   Both groups were somewhat socio-economically dispossessed.

4.)   All wanted an education for their teens.

5.)   Both groups had concerned parents although they had differences. The African American culture tended to be more matriarchal and Christian based while the Somali group was more patriarchal and Muslim based.

The solution the school developed was to establish parent meetings with the mothers and fathers of both groups to develop common goals. Each agreed to talk to their children about tolerance and respect and they agreed to help each other. As a result of the stabbing our school has become safer. We are looking forward this year to introduce meetings with translation for our Hispanic parents and Hmong parents. This is using the strength of the members to restore harmony in the group. If we only had first dealt with the offender as an individual problem it would have been a restitution payback with the boy taking a temper control class or even doing community service. The solution can be moved to a restitution pay forward when the staff students and parents begin to explore and solve the underlying issues for long term change.

DISTRICT WIDE CHANGE

Richfield Public Schools, Richfield, MN

Report On Responsibility Training

Richfield School District is ten minutes from the Minneapolis airport. It is a blue collar community with a diverse population of students. It is several blocks from the new Best Buy headquarters which houses 5000 employees. In the Richfield School's Strategic Plan for 1995-2000, Strategy Number III calls for the district to "develop and implement strategies to ensure a continued safe, supportive and caring environment." Richfield Schools have adopted the tenets of Responsibility Restitution Training/Control Theory (RT/CT) as a framework for helping to implement this strategy with their 450 employees.

Richfield Schools have been involved with the program since June of 1992 when the first training session was presented by Diane Gossen to a group of fifty administrators and teachers. The district has continued to consistently offer workshops and additional training to all staff. From the beginning, this was intended as a total-district program. Since 1993, more than 689 staff members have participated in a minimum of a ten hour workshop on this topic. Of this number, thirteen were administrators, 178 were classified staff (assistants, clerical, bus drivers, etc) and the remaining 498 were teaching staff. While many of those individuals have now left the district through moves and retirement, these figures speak to the ongoing commitment of resources and time to provide continuity for this program.

After five years, in a survey of the teaching staff in the fall of 1997, it was determined that 91% of the teaching staff had participated in at least twelve hours of training in RT/CT and approximately 30% had taken twelve to more than fifty hours of training. Since the fall of 1997, the district has offered, in house, eight additional sixteen hours Basic Workshops in which 118 staff have participated. Those attending included paraprofessionals, teachers and nine reserve teachers. There were five Parent Nights presented for parents from the total district to provide opportunities for them to learn more of the strategies being used in the schools. More then 300 parents attended these sessions. In May 2002, Nancy Rowley, board chair person of the Richfield School Board, proposed a motion that on the tenth anniversary of the first responsibility training the board recommit itself to the program. Each year new staff will continue to receive eighteen hours of in-service on student management.

Richfield High School with a staff of 80 teachers is the secondary program that has been using Restitution the longest time. In 1992, Teresa Rosen, assistant principal, and Bob Chemberlin, science teacher, began teaching the ideas through voluntary 45 minute meetings with colleagues every second week. Their partners with the Richfield police department also joined in. In the past decade the school went from 18% diversity to 37% diversity, but the incidence of discipline did not increase. Also Richfield District adopted four core beliefs that can be seen at the businesses and churches and recreation centers all over the community. Dr. Judy Anderson with Richfield staff also has developed a form for people to self evaluate their Restitution skills.

Prepared by Terri Robertson

Responsibility Training – Richfield School District
Self evaluation Survey

Place an "X" on each line indicating where you are on the continuum.

1.	I seldom self-evaluate, "Is what I'm doing aligned with what I want, know and believe?"					I frequently self-evaluate, "Is what I'm doing aligned with what I want, know and believe?"
2.	I mostly use consequences and/or rewards to solve problems with students.					I mostly work with students to solve problems.
3.	It's my job to make students be good and do their work.					It's my job to help students take responsibility for their work and behavior.
4.	I have a high number of class removals (ALPS, ISS, Office, etc.)					I have a low number of class removals (ALPS, ISS, Office, etc.)
5.	It's not okay to make a mistake.					It's okay to make a mistake.
6.	Everything matters.					I frequently ask myself, "Does it really matter?"
7.	I frequently say, "No."					I say, "Yes," or "Yes, if…" as often as possible.
8.	I solve students' problems.					My students solve their problems.
9.	I see misbehavior as bad.					I see misbehavior as purposeful.
10.	I frequently say, "What will happen to me?" or "What do I get?"					I frequently say, "Am I being the kind of person I want to be?"
11.	My students frequently say, "What will happen to me?" or "What do I get?"					My students frequently ask themselves, "Am I being the kind of person I want to be?"
12.	I focus on the problem.					I focus on the solution.
13.	I seldom use Control Theory principles to manage my stress.					I frequently use Control Theory principles to manage my stress.
14.	In a group I prefer voting and majority rule.					In a group I prefer consensus decision making.
15.	When students report problems, I say, "Who did it?" and "What happened?"					When students report problems, I say, "What did you do to solve the problem?" and "What could you do next time?"
16.	I seldom use research and best knowledge to plan.					I usually use best knowledge and research to plan.

Restitution Schools Report

#						
17.	My students hide their mistakes, blame others, deny or make up excuses.					My students are honest and open, and accept responsibility for their behavior.
18.	After discussing a problem with me, I think the person goes away with a failure identity.					After discussing a problem with me, I think the person goes away with a success identity.
19.	At a conference for a student having difficulty, I focus on the problem behaviors.					At a conference for a student having difficulty, I focus on the needs of the student.
20.	I focus on rules.					I focus on beliefs and values.
21.	I develop the classroom rules and expectations.					My students and I together develop a classroom agreement
22.	I hear myself say, "It was your fault."					I hear myself say, "This was my part of the problem."
23.	I get stuck on the back wheels of my behavior car (feelings and physiology).					I can move from the back wheels to the front wheels of my behavior car (move from feelings to thinking and action).
24.	I say to myself and others, "You should have done better!"					I say to myself and others, "Could you have done worse?"
25.	I have little input in important decisions in my school.					I have significant impact in important decisions in my school.
26.	I do not see discipline as part of my job. Teaching the curriculum is my job.					I see discipline as part of my job. Part of the curriculum is building a caring community, teaching problem solving skills, and teaching control theory.
27.	I am usually a punisher or a guilter.					I am usually a monitor or a manager.
28.	I avoid conflict.					I see conflict as an opportunity to grow.
29.	I seldom ask people what they want.					I frequently ask people what they want, and how I can help them get some of what they need.
30.	When people complain, I commiserate with them or try to convince them that it's not so bad.					When people complain, I say to them, "Do you just want me to listen to you complain, or do you want to talk about a solution?"
31.	I focus on convincing other people of my point of view.					I focus on understanding other people's perceptions.

Saanich School District, Saanichton, BC

The Saanich School District #63 began its journey with Restitution in 1998. Barrie Bennett, of the Ontario Institute for Studies in Education of the University of Toronto worked with the Saanich District for three years in Instructional Strategies. Barrie shared two pieces of a puzzle that equates to student success: Instructional Strategies and Relationships. This reverberated with a district staff member who had pursued training in Control Theory and Restitution.

Restitution has become a common approach that many schools in Saanich are exploring and teachers are implementing in their classrooms. The evolution of Restitution within the district followed the process as described in *Creating the Conditions: Leadership for Quality Schools* (Judy Anderson and Diane Gossen, 1996):

- **Cognitive change**: Information on Control Theory and Restitution was shared with the District Professional Growth Council, district administrators, executive, district trustees, school staffs and individuals. District has worked extensively staying current with brain-research and character education material written/presented by such authors as Alfie Kohn, Eric Jensen, William Glasser, Barrie Bennett, Rushworth Kidder, William Powers and Diane Gossen. Staff read *Restitution, Restructuring School Discipline* through book clubs, professional development and various work groups

- **Personal change**: People began to question our stimulus-response practices. The Saanich District has provided five Level I and two Level II training sessions, various work sessions and community forums sharing the ideas of Restitution. Presently, over 250 district employees Administrators, teachers, teaching assistants, teacher substitutes, university intern students, parents, Restorative Justice members and First Nation participants have had training.

- **System Change**: Network and dialogue occurred at district and school levels to explore beliefs and construct social contracts. Staffs began implementation of the ideas. A Restitution support group was formed where teachers could meet to collaborate, share experiences and practise skills. Visits to classrooms were made by the district's Restitution facilitator to teach and model the ideas of Control Theory and Restitution.

- **Culture Change**: School wide dialogue began to take place where staffs examined relationships; student-to-student, student to adult, adult to student and adult-to-adult. This opened up the territory towards reflection and self evaluation leading to improved conflict resolution awareness and practise. All elementary administrators spent a day looking at British Columbia's Performance Standards for Social Responsibility, examining research comparing didactic vs. holistic approaches to address Social Responsibility and using the ideas of Restitution.

- **Program change**: Schools began to change by exploring how their practices aligned with their beliefs. Schools were able to identify where things were working well and where efforts could be made to improve.

- **Continual change**: Five years moving towards becoming a Restitution district, the process of self- evaluation and practise continues.

CREATING THE CONDITIONS

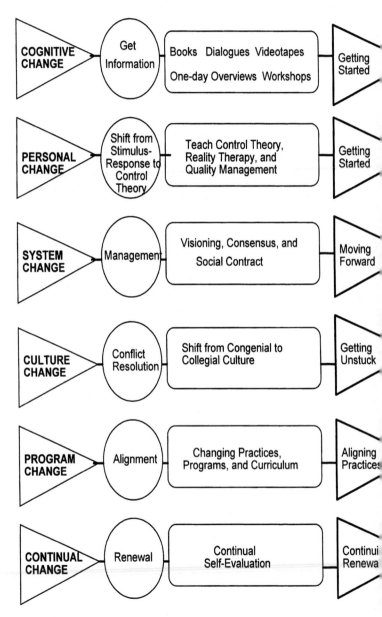

COGNITIVE CHANGE	Get Information	Books Dialogues Videotapes One-day Overviews Workshops	Getting Started
PERSONAL CHANGE	Shift from Stimulus-Response to Control Theory	Teach Control Theory, Reality Therapy, and Quality Management	Getting Started
SYSTEM CHANGE	Management	Visioning, Consensus, and Social Contract	Moving Forward
CULTURE CHANGE	Conflict Resolution	Shift from Congenial to Collegial Culture	Getting Unstuck
PROGRAM CHANGE	Alignment	Changing Practices, Programs, and Curriculum	Aligning Practices
CONTINUAL CHANGE	Renewal	Continual Self-Evaluation	Continui Renewa

Adapted from CBAM, Gene Hall from the University of Texas

Restitution Schools Report

Saanich is committed to providing continued opportunities for training. Individual teachers and schools are witnessing the positive results. Teachers have shared that they are not working as hard and feel healthier as a result. Students have a greater knowledge about behavior through learning about the needs. Teachers share that they have to work less to control and students are becoming more socially responsible based on greater intrinsic values. They are becoming better managers of their behavior. A grade four teacher shares, "The first week of school the children were 'wild' and I knew I had to do something different to maintain my sanity for a whole year. I made the decision to spend time developing class beliefs, Y-charts for respect and 'My Job/Your Job' while many of my colleagues went straight into academics. I talked to the principal about the guilt I was feeling for not teaching reading, writing and math. She replied, "Sometimes you need to go slow to move faster later." The teacher continues," It was great relief to hear that and I ran with it. Within a few weeks, I noticed a huge difference in the tone of the class. I don't nag at them which makes me feel a lot better about my job. The class doesn't come from a position of tattling because now we solve problems; not blame or shame."

Two grade eight girls, were referred due to skipping a P.E. class and arrived late to a Home Economic classroom instead. The class was interrupted while the teacher looked for their names on the register. The girls worked with the Restorative Justice team who introduced the needs to the two students. They quickly identified fun as their need. Their behaviour was to skip "boring" physical education and have some "fun." The girls recognized the inconvenience their actions had on the Home Economics' class. The girls identified a plan of Restitution and upon completion of their plan stated,

"This Restitution is a lot better than punishment. Restitution makes you think more before doing... punishment just makes people mad, whereas Restitution, you repair.... and go on."

This testimony is just one of many that have been shared throughout the district. There is greater clarity between adults, students and parents as a result of our journey in Restitution. It has helped us to verify assumptions and improved our consensus building at the intra-personal, inter-personal and systems levels. What we know is that the levels and degree of diversity in our population is ever increasing. Of this we have no control. What we do have control over is the manner in which we as individuals and systems, respond to our changing social norms. The Saanich district remains committed in our evolution and practice in Restitution. Our journey from traditional means of discipline, extrinsic control and conformity, towards a needs satisfying environment void of coercion and fear is making a difference.

Teachers are expressing greater job satisfaction and seeing a difference in students. We feel that Restitution truly represents our values and beliefs rooted in the concepts of internal motivation. This will better provide students the necessary knowledge and skills to be socially responsible citizens. The following is a rubric we created to meet our social responsibility criteria through Restitution.

John Martin
Instructional Support-Student Services
Saanich School District #63

Saanich Restitution Rubric

	1	2	3	4	Evaluation
Character education	Rules-based No recognition of underlying values/beliefs	Values are evident but directed by adults "to children"	Open dialogue with students to construct common values	Behavior and language reflects intrinsic ownership and responsibility	
Rewards	Punishment orientation for negative behavior	Positive rewards for good behavior e.g. points for pizza	Adult support and monitoring to guide more intrinsically driven behavior	Students rewarded by intrinsic motivation "being the people they want to be"	
Mistakes	Student mistakes are isolated, identified and shared as negative examples	Mistakes identified but counseling occurs in a more private manner	Adult provide a "plan" to support student's attempt to "fix" the mistake	Students recognize and own mistakes and initiate a plan of restitution	
Adult relationships	Talk about each other behind their backs	Varying opinions heard but disregarded in consequent actions	Courteous toward each other but not a shared vision	All adults communicate and treat each other with respect through shared vision	

Restitution at Hampton-Dumont Community School District
Hampton, Iowa

Many of our elementary teachers at Hampton-Dumont use Restitution in their classrooms, at recess, and in their personal lives. I am speaking from an elementary viewpoint. In 1994, a climate/culture study was done in our school system sponsored by our local area education agency and it was determined that the climate and culture of our buildings needs some improvement. Conflicts in and out of the classroom were a major concern. Teachers felt that much of their time was spent punishing or putting out fires rather than concentrating on teaching.

After the study we started a conflict resolution program that focused on training all students rather than just a select few. The program worked well, but staff felt like something was missing. After the students determined what the conflict was and what they both needed to be happy, they were stuck. They needed to see things from a different point of view. Restitution was the answer.

Restitution has changed lives at Hampton-Dumont. Restitution trainings have had a profound impact on the way teachers look at the behaviors of others and how they respond. The role of the teacher has become much more important because they are teaching the life skills required to get along in society rather than just handing down punishment sentences to 'put out fires' along the way.

Change has not been easy. The teachers that use Restitution like to schedule times to get together and dialogue about Restitution ideas on a regular basis. Without that, it is too easy to slip back into old approaches. The results make the change worthwhile. In the classroom, students have learned to separate the person from the behavior and are helping each other as they acquire the skills. They have determined that the teacher is not going to fix the problem or simply punish the person with whom they have a conflict. Instead, they use a combination of their conflict resolution skills and Restitution to 'make it right." Teachers hope that these skills will carry over into their lives at home and in the future.

Restitution gives students an 'out' or a chance to 'save face'. Students don't feel the need to lie because they understand that they made a mistake, everyone one makes mistakes, and that they will feel more in control if they own up to it and then fix it. It teaches students how our emotions control how our brain works or doesn't work (brain stem) and then it teaches them how to get around those roadblocks. Restitution empowers students, builds confidence, and creates positive thinking.

Student and substitute teachers report back to homeroom teachers that they are amazed at the decreased amount of tattling in the classrooms that use Restitution. Students can work through problems together before they have to come to the teacher for help. There have been other benefits in the teacher's personal lives as well. Staff reports that there is a 'calmer' feeling to the way that they approach conflict. Restitution has helped them to deal with the issues at hand and to stay on track. They are now standing beside and not in front when dealing with a situation. They are shoulder-to-shoulder, not toe-to-toe.

To keep Restitution alive, it is important to have a few key people in your district, including some parents. It is extremely helpful if the administration is on board. We try to provide as many opportunities for training as we can, including making sure that all new staff have received training in at least Restitution I. We also try to provide as many opportunities as possible to refresh ideas during staff meeting, book studies, watching the Restitution tapes again. On a yearly basis, we also provide parent groups to discuss Restitution, how we use it at school and how that can carry over into the home. We had one parent meeting where there were one hundred and thirty parents. Each one was given the book, *My Child Is A Pleasure*.

One veteran teacher reported to me her experience with Restitution.
"I've taught school for 32 years and this works better and makes more sense than anything I've ever done. Students listen when I respectfully talk with them about 'what kind of person do you want to be' and 'what that will look like'. Teaching control theory and Restitution has helped me understand not only my students, but also all people better. It helps me personally analyze my own needs and meet them in appropriate ways."
Submitted by: Sheryl Borcherding
        Elementary Guidance Counselor and Restitution Facilitator

EAU CLAIRE AREA SCHOOL DISTRICT
Eau Claire, WI

When I came to the Eau Claire Areas School District (ECASD) in 1999 staff members were asking for more information about Restitution Self Discipline. In the early 90's a regional alternative school, the Eau Claire County Off Campus School, had heard Diane Gossen speak and began adopting her model. In 1996 McKinley Charter School and a few interested staff from throughout the district began using the Restitution model. Being new to the district, my first questions were "Is there district-wide interest in moving towards a common discipline model and was there funding to do so?

Administrators were asked to complete self assessment surveys and determine the level of interest among the staff in their buildings. The ECASD serves 10,000 students in two highs schools, 3 middle schools, 12 elementary schools, and 3 charter schools. Administrators and student services staff were invited to attend informational sessions with Diane to learn more about the program. Funding was secured through multiple AODA grants.

Our first district training session was held in the summer of 2000 for 80 staff members. From the very beginning the #1 question from building staff was "Are all district staff going to be 'required' to take training and implement restitution?" The answer has always been the same "Restitution is being offered to allow staff to gather new information about a discipline model being offered to create a needs satisfying environment for all students and staff." Staff will not be "required" to attend. Since this time Restitution has gained momentum purely on the merits of the program itself.

The first three years of implementation were merely to offer enough training to develop a mass of individuals within buildings, to foster a love of learning for the restitution and control theory principles (cognitive change). Staffs were encouraged to try out what they learned at home and in the classroom (personal change). To move any faster than this, in a district our size, would have destroyed the passion that individuals had for the program. During the last year and a half we began to see a system change and a culture change in a few of our buildings that are using Restitution as a means to achieve Continuous Improvement Model goals in their buildings.

More and more people are talking about Restitution in the classroom. Curriculum units have been developed to teach restitution concepts at all levels...principal to staff, staff to students, students to students, and staff to parents. At our first parent night in 2000 we had 5 people attend. At our last one in January of 2004 we had 65 people attend. As I walk down the halls of our various school buildings I have staff stop me and tell me their stories. I hear how Restitution has improved their interactions with family members, staff, and students. They show me the tools they have created to use in the classroom and on the playground to help the students. I have had teachers who have been in the field of education for over 20 years express a renewed sense of spirit in the field of education as they implement new strategies to work with today's students. Here is an example:

> I then tell my students that in my classroom I will present them with
> problems to solve. I will give them guidelines which clearly state
> the purpose and objective of each lesson; however, every experience
> will allow room for them to be an individual and no two solutions

need be the same. Each problem I tell them will allow each of them to invest something of their selves in it. Furthermore, they have a choice on how they view each learning experience. They can view it a something they have to do to avoid getting a bad grade or the disapproval of their teacher/ parent or they can view it as an opportunity to stretch and grow as an individual and as an artist.

Prior to Restitution training, I looked at the field of school administration and thought discipline would be the hardest part of the job. Personally I didn't feel fear and coercion were the most effective means to deal with student behavior. Now, five years later, I feel that with the use of restitution concepts, determining shared values and beliefs, establishing mutually agreed upon bottom lines, and creating a culture of mutual respect for self and others discipline is a manageable part of administration and teaching.

Every building in our district is at a different level in the implementation of Restitution, and that's OK. We are building a core of staff that are becoming experts in restitution and will serve as mentors for new staff. Restitution is a personal journey, as well as a professional one. It is a constantly evolving process by which we can continually renew our skills needed to work with youth in today's ever changing society. I close by sharing the self assessment form we created to evaluate Restitution.

Submitted by;
Jean Schroeder Christenson
ATOD Prevention Coordinator

Restitution Self Assessment Survey

	I have little or no knowledge about this strategy and no plans to use the strategy	I am gathering information about this strategy through reading discussions, observations, and/or workshops	I have established a time to begin implementing this strategy	I am using the strategy . . . preliminary phase	I routinely use this strategy, and I am satisfied with how the strategy is being implemented	I use this strategy, and I'm beginning to modify its implementation to enhance the strategy's impact on students	I use this strategy, and I am working with colleagues to combine my efforts with theirs to achieve a collective impact on our students
Using the 5 positions of control to assess classroom management style							
Develop and use of social contract in classroom							
Develop my job/your job with students							
Teaching the needs to students							
Using the reality therapy questions							

© Jean Christenson

Restitution Peace Project Description and Evaluation Approach - Yellowknife, NT

The Restitution Peace Project is an ambitious 1.5 million dollar four-year initiative to implement Restitution and Control Theory in ten community schools in the Northwest Territories and Nunavut, from 2002-2006. It is funded primarily by the National Crime Prevention Centre, Justice Canada and is sponsored by Yellowknife Education District No.1 and community partners under the guidance of the Project Steering Committee. There are two full-time employed staff who coordinate all aspects of the project – Lynn Taylor and Arlene Bell. The project is being researched by an independent, third party evaluator – Tim Roberts of Focus Consultants, Victoria, B.C., with the support of a national evaluation advisory committee.

The ten project site schools are located in the communities of Yellowknife, Hay River Reserve, Fort McPherson, Inuvik, and Aklavik in the Northwest Territories; and Cambridge Bay, Rankin Inlet, and Iqaluit in Nunavut. Information was sent out inviting schools across the North to participate. Schools in these communities rose to the challenge, applied and were accepted into the project.

The project is a unique educational, social development approach for crime prevention, designed primarily for teachers, children, and parents, as well as community members as a whole. Elders, parents, counsellors, RCMP, corrections staff, justice committees, safe-shelter employees, treatment centre caregivers, business people, politicians, as well as educators from pre-school through college level have participated in project training sessions. This is the first broad-based restorative project of its kind in the North with a goal to help create and support the development of "A Connected Community."

The purpose of the project is:

- To teach educators, parents and community caregivers new skills and strategies to work with youth.
- To create school environments that are caring, achieving, and safe.
- To teach adults and children to manage themselves by meeting their needs in helpful ways, to repair their mistakes, and to develop internal character strength.
- To develop an educational framework and resource base for training Northerners to ensure program continuity and long-term sustainability.
- To improve the low rate of high school graduates in the North.
- To help address youth and family violence problems.
- To respond to a growing concern for safer schools and communities.

The project has some unique challenges:

- The enormous geographical area spans over three million square kilometres across the Northwest Territories and Nunavut. Site schools stretch from the shores of Frobisher Bay in the North Atlantic in the east, to the mighty Mackenzie River Delta near the Beaufort Sea in the west, to Dease Straight in the Arctic Ocean in the north, to the shores of Great Slave Lake in the south, and to the central Hudson Bay area. Traveling vast distances by air and road from tree line to tundra in inclement arctic weather can be unpredictable as well as exciting!

- There are eight official languages spoken in the Northwest Territories and Nunavut – more than any other political division in Canada, plus additional dialects in several of the language groups. Some project resources have been translated into Inuktitut, Inuinnaqtun, and French. In the eastern arctic some schools have to provide Inuktitut translators for the training sessions for their staff and parents.

Many individuals have generously contributed their time and expertise to help this project be successful: Mike Bell, Steering Committee Chairperson; Committee members Nancy Galway, John Howard Society; Barbara Saunders and staff, NWT Status of Women Council; Judith Knapp, Superintendent of Yellowknife Education District No.1 and staff; Guenther Laube, Director of the National Crime Prevention Centre Northern Region; Adrian Papanek and Monty Pittson, National Crime Prevention Centre, Ottawa; Jeff Grumley, mentor/trainer/author/researcher; Diane Gossen, Restitution program developer/trainer/author; Jackie Eaton, resource coordinator; Shelley Brierley, Bruce Innes, Judy Anderson, Ted Amendt and Yves Bousquet, Restitution Trainers; Tim Roberts and Doris McCann of Focus Consultants; members of the Evaluation Advisory Committee; and last but not least, the principals, committee members and staff of all the site schools. A project of this scale is only possible due to the combined efforts of the people involved. Everyone's commitment and support has been significant and is greatly appreciated!

The Restitution Peace Project Overview

Restitution means "making things better" and differs from the criminal justice definition of payback. Restitution is a program based on respect and common beliefs that builds community, empowers individuals, and resolves conflict. It offers knowledge and skills for educators, parents, and community helpers to respectfully work with children in a safe, non-coercive environment to help them learn self-discipline and become productive, principled citizens. This restorative approach helps people understand why they behave and provides problem-solving skills that strengthen people as they learn to fix their mistakes, repair relationships, and return to balance. Self-discipline results in improved self-esteem, better relationships, and increased achievement. In schools where Restitution is implemented, discipline incidents decline, school attendance increases, grades improve, and students, staff and parents enjoy a more caring school community.

Aboriginal people will recognize many of the ideas that are behind the Restitution Program, which emphasizes belonging, mastery, independence, and generosity.

École J.H. Sissons School in Yellowknife was the first NWT school to implement the Restitution program several years ago, creating the "Peace Circle Model" as a Northern prototype. This model offers a process for schools to change from an external "rewards and punishments" discipline system, to a restorative, belief-based system where basic needs are met, internal motivation is fostered, and responsible decision-making results. A video documenting the school's journey is available on the website, www.RestitutionNorth.ca.

Decline in Major Behavior Incidents at École J.H. Sissons

Year	1998-1999 Started Restitution Oct. 1998	1999 - 2000	2000- 2001	2001- 2002	2002- 2003
In-School Suspensions	Approx. 49	9	7	3	1
Out-of-School Suspensions	incidents combined	33	27	5	7
Total Suspensions	49	42	34	8	8

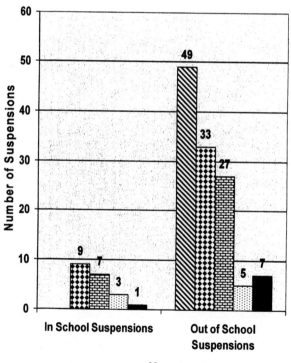

Purpose of the Restitution Peace Project: May '02 to April '06

➤ To teach educators, parents and community caregivers new skills and strategies to work with youth and create need-satisfying environments.

➤ To teach children to manage themselves by meeting their needs in helpful ways and to repair their mistakes, thereby developing internal character strength.

➤ To develop an educational framework and resource base for training Northerners to ensure program continuity and long-term sustainability.

➤ To help address the lower than average rate of high school graduates in the North. (NWT high school graduation rate is 50% overall, and 26% in the Aboriginal population compared to 75% overall in Canada.)

➤ To help address youth and family violence problems.

➤ To respond to a growing concern for safer schools and communities. (Stats Can indicates that the NWT has the highest per capita rate of incarceration in Canada with convictions for violent crime at 5 times the national average and 6 times for sexual assault. Heavy alcohol consumption is twice the national average, and the use of family shelters is 8 times higher than the rest of Canada.)

How Restitution, Effective Behavioural Support (EBS), and Character Education Programs can complement each other

EBS provides a whole-school monitoring process to develop a common framework for standards, expectations, and supportive environments.

Character education programs support children's social and moral development through teaching positive human values or virtues to encourage ethical character growth.

The Restitution program builds upon an external monitoring process (such as EBS), incorporates ideas and vocabulary for best-self concept (such as Character Ed), and proceeds further to develop a self-managing approach which is based on internal motivation. This paves the way for students and staff to become self-disciplined. Restitution applies to both the individual and the whole school. This restorative program is based on respect and common beliefs that strengthen individuals and build community. It helps people understand that they are internally motivated, that their behaviour is purposeful, and provides problem-solving strategies to help students collapse conflict and look within. This develops character strength and a success identity in students.

Yellowknife Education District No.1 and the Steering Committee are the sponsors.

A ripple of northern lights, respect, the restorative restitution triangle and the all-embracing circle of community are symbolized in the project logo.

The National Crime Prevention Centre Canada is funding the project.

The Restitution Peace Project spans the Northwest Territories and Nunavut with eleven schools in eight northern communities participating.

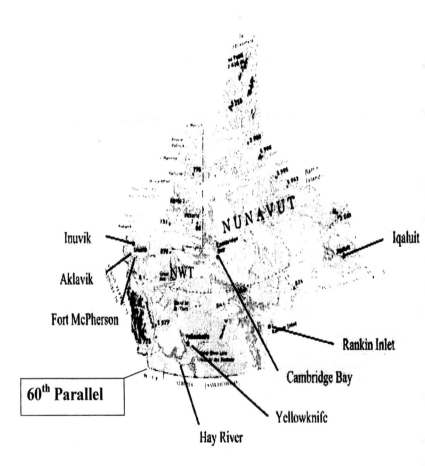

Inuvik

Aklavik

Fort McPherson

60th Parallel

Hay River

NUNAVUT

NWT

Iqaluit

Rankin Inlet

Cambridge Bay

Yellowknife

R.P.P. Program Analysis – Program Objectives

Program Objective	Evaluation Process Issues
Implement restitution process in 10 school sites	Administrative structure and support
	Site solicitation; schools' decision to participate
	Location and number of schools
	Extent to which restitution implemented in each school; factors constraining or facilitating implementation
Develop a restitution committee at each site to guide and support the process.	Whether established; membership and activities
	Effectiveness
Develop effective partnerships that will help to sustain restitution program after end of demonstration project.	Partnerships developed; type of involvement
	Factors helping/hindering long-term sustainability
Ensure steps to secure alternative sources of funding once Agreement terminated	Whether strategy for alternative funding has been developed
Build a delivery structure for restitution training and support.	Training and support provided
	Quality of trainers and of training
	Adequacy of RPP support and communication
	Development of a Northern-based training capacity
Develop resources and support materials to sustain restitution program and create links with existing curriculum	Extent, cultural relevance and adequacy of materials created
	Creation of links with aboriginal curriculum
Facilitate the transfer of skills to parents and families	Types of outreach to parents; underlying strategy

Submitted by Lynn Taylor
Restitution Peace Project Coordinator

Evergreen School District ABC Plan Survey
Vancouver, WA

Evergreen is the fastest growing district in Washington state and it is to their credit that they have held the edge of change. Evergreen School District is located in Southwest Washington and is the home for 24,000 students and over 2500 staff. It covers 54 square miles and has a population of over 95,000. Currently, there are 28 schools. Our belief is that only a collaborative effort of all staff, students and the community can create true change in schools. For this reason, we have chosen a systems model for our continued journey toward quality. Over five years we trained all staff members, both clerical and credentialed in the ideas of Control Theory and Restitution. In 2002 Evergreen School District received the first William and Melissa Gates Grant of $9.2 million to reinvent the high school of the future. There follows a survey that we did to assess the implementation level after five years. Our training is called Responsible Decision Making.

Goal: To create a positive environment in which to learn and work, where students and staff are valued, and where all stakeholders are invested in the success of our students. I have taken a 3-day overview workshop from Diane Gossen.   695 - Yes   93 - No

I use the following strategies of Responsibility Decision Making (RDM) in my classroom. Mark all that apply.

My Job/Your Job -	652 (93%)
Behavior Car	177 (25%)
Classroom Beliefs	566 (81%)
Restitution	536 (77%)

Basic Needs	547 (78%)
What's Your Plan	549 (78%)
None	23 (0.03%

I use the concepts of RDM in my classroom.

Occasionally	177 (25%)
Daily	419 (60%)
Weekly	103 (14%)
Do not use	48 (0.06%)

My staff has spent time discussing and implementing the district EXPECTATIONS (beliefs) (how much time)?

2 hours - 369   8 hours - 194   12 hours - 115

**Implementation By Teachers Five Years After Training
695 Surveyed - Evergreen School District, Vancouver, WA**

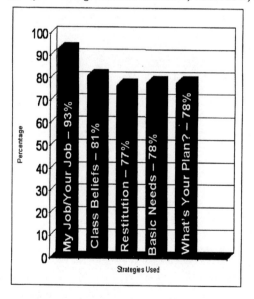

The following is an outline of the Evergreen five year plan for Responsible Decision Making (Control Theory) and Restitution.

CARING CULTURE

C4	All employees will apply Responsible Decision Making (RDM) processes in their duties and responsibilities.	• Each employee of the district will complete an overview of RDM. • Follow up training sessions will be available annually including opportunities for Basic Intensive Week and Basic Practicum. • Each staff member will self evaluate their use and knowledge of RDM and co-verify it with their supervisor.
C5	All employees working with students will apply the Restitution process in carrying out their duties and responsibilities.	• All employees working with students will complete an overview of Restitution.
C6	All students of the district will have a basic understanding of Responsible Decision Making (RDM) and be able to apply it in the school environment.	• RDM will be integrated into the existing curriculum as developmentally appropriate.
C7	Parents of students in the district and other community members will be provided information on RDM/Expectations.	• Information on RDM/Expectations will be included in the district's communication annually. • Training seminars in RDM/Expectations will be offered in the fall, winter, and spring annually.
C8	All employees within the district will interact with each other in accordance with the district Expectations.	• Each employee of the district will develop a personalized plan for living the Expectations. • The evaluation system for all managers and supervisors will reflect their progress in meeting the district Expectations and shall be reviewed annually.

	MEASURABLE RESULT	97-98	98-99	99-00
C4	• By December 31, 1997, each employee will have completed a three-day overview of RDM.	X		
	• Within 12 months after being hired, new staff will complete a three-day overview of RDM.	X	X	X
	• By June 30 of each year, follow-up sessions will have been offered.	X	X	X
	• Annually, staff evaluations will reflect his/her use and application of RDM.	X	X	X
C5	• By June 30, 1999, all instructional management staff and counselors will have completed a two-day overview of Restitution.		X	
	• By June 30, 2000, all staff working directly with students will have completed a two-day overview of Restitution, as evidenced by training records in the Staff Development Office.			X
C6	• By June 30, 1998, the Curriculum/Restructuring Office will develop and have on file a plan for how to add and/or integrate RDM into existing curriculum frameworks.	X		
	• By June 30, 1999, the RDM student plan will have been implemented.		X	
	• By June 30, 2000, data/evidence will be collected to assess how RDM is being applied by students at the classroom level.			X
C7	• Each year by June 30, information on RDM/Expectations will be contained in district communications on file in the Community Relations Office.	X	X	X
	• Each year by June 30, three training seminars in RDM/Expectations will have been offered, as evidenced by enrollment records available in the Community Education Office.	X	X	X
C8	• Annually, all employees will develop an expectation plan and will have reviewed his/her progress with his/her supervisor.	X	X	X
	• References to the Expectations will be reflected in the evaluative comments for managers and supervisors.	X	X	X
	• By June 30 of each year, the Instructional Planning Team will review the implementation of the Expectations process.	X	X	X

LIST OF RESOURCES

If you are interested in pursuing these ideas through further study, you may want to explore some of the following materials:

Anderson, Judy & Gossen, Diane. *Creating the Conditions: Leadership for Quality Schools*. Chapel Hill: New View, 1996.

Baldwin, Christina. *Calling the Cirlce: The First and Future Culture.* Newberg: Swan Raven & Co. 1994.

Bell, David. *Sharing Our Success: Ten Case Studies in Aboriginal Schooling*, Kelowna: Society for the Advancement of Excellence in Education, 2004.

Boffey, Barnes. *Reinventing Yourself.* Chapel Hill: New View Publications, 1993.

Brendtro, Larry, Martin Brokenleg and Steve Van Bockern. *Reclaiming Youth At Risk: Our Hope for the Future*. Bloomington: National Educational Service, 1990.

Brown, Willow. *Building A Learning Community Through Restitution: A Case Study.* Saskatoon: University of Saskatchewan, 2004.

Caine, R. N., and G. Caine. *Education on the Edge of Possibility.* Alexandria, VA, ASCD, 1997.

Caine, R. N., and G. Caine, *Unleashing the Power of Perceptual Change: The Potential of Brain-Based Teaching*, Alexandria: Association for Supervision and Curriculum Development, 1997.

Charney, Ruth Sidney. *Teaching Children to Care: Management in the Responsive Classroom.* Greenfield: Northeast Foundation for Children, 1992.

Covey, Stephen R. *Principle-Centered Leadership.* New York: Summit Books, 1990.

Covey, Stephen R. *The Seven Habits of Highly Effective People: Restoring the Character Ethic.* New York: Simon & Schuster, 1989.

Curwin, Richard L. and Allen N. Mendler. *As Tough As Necessary: Countering Aggression and Hostility in Our Schools* . Alexandria: Association for Supervision and Curriculum Development, 1997.

Curwin, Richard L. and Allen N. Mendler. *Discipline With Dignity*. Alexandria: Association for Supervision and Curriculum Development, 1988.

De Becker, Gavin. *Protecting the Gift: Keeping Children and Teenagers Safe (and Parents Sane).* New York: Dell Publishing, 1999.

Deci, Edward L. & Richard Flaste. *Why We Do What We Do.* New York: Penguin Books, 1996.

DePorter, Bobbi and Mark Reardon, Sarah Singer-Nourie. *Quantum Teaching: Orchestrating Student Success.* Needham Heights: Allyn & Bacon, 1999.

Erwin, Jonathan C. *The Classroom of Choice: Giving Students What They Need and Getting What You Want.* Alexandria: Association for Supervision and Curriculum Development, 2004.

Freiberg, H. Jerome. *Beyond Behaviorism: Changing Classroom Management Paradigm.* Needham Heights: Allyn and Bacon, 1999.

Fritz, Robert. *The Path of Least Resistance for Managers: Designing Organizations to Succeed.* San Francisco: Berrett-Koehler Publishers, 1999.

Glasser, Wm. M.D. *Choice Theory.* New York: HarperCollins Publishers, 1998.

Glasser, Wm. M.D. *Control Theory.* New York: Harper & Row, 1984.

Glasser, Wm. M.D. *Reality Therapy.* New York: Harper & Row, 1965.

Glasser, Wm. M.D. *Schools Without Failure.* New York: Harper & Row, 1969.

Glasser, Wm. M.D. *The Quality School.* New York: Harper & Row, 1990.

Glasser, Wm. M.D. *The Quality School Teacher.* New York: Harper & Row, 1993.

Glickman, Carl D. *Renewing America's Schools: A Guide for School-Based Education.* San Francisco: Jossey-Bass Publishers, 1993.

Gilligan, James, M.D. *Reflections On A National Epidemic: Violence.* New York: Vintage Books, 1997.

Goleman, Daniel. *Emotional Intelligence: Why It Can Matter More Than IQ.* New York: Bantam Books, 1995.

Good, E. Perry Good, Jeff Grumley, Shelley Roy. *A Connected School,* Chapel Hill: New View, 2003.

Good, E. Perry. *Helping Kids Help Themselves.* Chapel Hill: New View Publications, 1992.

Good, E. Perry. *In Pursuit of Happiness.* Chapel Hill: New View Publications, 1987.

Gossen, Diane, Ed. *Building A Quality School.* Saskatoon: Chelsom Consultants Limited, 1996.

Gossen, Diane, Ed. *Class Meetings.* Saskatoon: Chelsom Consultants Limited, 1988.

Gossen, Diane. *Control Theory in Action.* Saskatoon: Chelsom Consultants Limited, 1995.

Gossen, Diane, Ed. *Don't Fight Make It Right.* Saskatoon: Chelsom Consultants Limited, 2000.

Gossen, Diane. *Heal the Hurt.* Saskatoon: Chelsom Consultants Limited, 1999.

Gossen, Diane. The Person I Want To Be. Saskatoon: Chelsom Consultants Limited, 1995.

Gossen, Diane. *Many Faces of Change.* Saskatoon: Chelsom Consultants Limited, 1996.

Gossen, Diane. *My Child Is A Pleasure.* Saskatoon: Chelsom Consultants Limited, 1988.

Gossen, Diane. *Restitution: Restructuring School Discipline.* Chapel Hill: New View Publications, 1992.

Gossen, Diane. *Restitution: Restructuring School Discipline Facilitator's Guide.* Chapel Hill: New View Publications, 1993.

Gossen, Diane. *Restitution For Teens.* Saskatoon: Chelsom Consultants Limited, 2000.

Gossen, Diane. *The Restitution Triangle.* Saskatoon: Chelsom Consultants Limited, 1996.

Gossen, Diane. *Self Designing Discipline.* Saskatoon: Chelsom Consultants Limited, 2000 .

Greene, Brad. *New Paradigms for Creating Quality Schools.* Chapel Hill: New View Publications, 1994.

Grossman, Lt. Col. Dave. *On Killing: The Psychological Cost of Learning to Kill in War and Society.* New York: Little Brown and Company, 1995.

Grossman, Lt. Col. Dave. *Stop Teaching Our Kids To Kill: A Call To Action Against TV, Movie & Video Game Violence.* New York: Little Brown and Company, 1995.

Hart, Linda and Kathy Wilson. *Parenting Is A Pleasure.* Saskatoon: Chelsom Consultants Ltd, 2001.

Hjálmarsson, Magni, Translator. Gossen, Diane. *Uppeldi til ábyrgdar: Olikar leidir, Spurt og svarad, Uppbyggingarprihornid.* Reyjavik: Islensk pyding, 2002.

Jensen, Eric. *Teaching With the Brain In Mind.* Alexandria: Association for Supervision and Curriculum Development, 1998.

Kessler, Rachael. *The Soul of Education: Helping Students Find Connection, Compassion and Character at School.* Alexandria: Association for Supervision and Curriculum Development, 2000.

Kelly, Jennifer. *The Road to Success – Thesis. Saint Paul: Hamline University, 1999.*

Kohn, Alfie. *Beyond Discipline.* Alexandria: Association for Supervision and Curriculum Development, 1996.

Kohn, Alfie. *Punished By Reward.* Houghton Mifflin Company, 1993.

Kohn, Alfie. *No Contest: The Case Against Competition.* Houghton Mifflin, 1992.

Kohn, Alfie. *The Brighter Side of Human Nature: Altruism and Empathy in Everyday Life.* Basic Books, 1990.

Kohn, Alfie, *The Schools Our Children Deserve: Moving Beyond Traditional Classrooms and "Tougher Standards",* 2002.

Larson, Scott & Larry Brendtro, *Reclaiming Our Prodigal Sons and Daughters: A Practical Approach for Connecting With Youth in Conflict,* Bloomington: National Educational Service, 2000.

Marken, Richard S. *More Mind Readings: Methods and Models in the Study of Purpose.* St. Louis: New View, 2002.

Marzano, Robert. Classroom Management That Works, Alexandria: Association for Supervision and Curriculum Development, 2003.

Palmer, Parker J. *Let Your Life Speak: Listening for the Voice of Vocation.* San Francisco: John Wiley and Sons, Inc., 2000.

Pert, Candace. *Molecules of Emotion: The Science Behind Mind-Body Medicine.* New York: Touchstone, 1997.

Pollack, William, Ph.D. *Real Boys: Rescuing Our Sons From the Myths of Boyhood.* New York: Henry Holt and Company, Inc, 1999.

Kavelin-Popov, Linda. *The Virtues Project Educator's Guide: Simple Ways to Create a Culture of Character.* Jalmar Press, 2000.

Powers, William. *Behavior the Control of Perception.* Chicago: Aldine de Gruyter, 1973.

Powers, William. *Living Control Systems.* Kentucky: The Control Systems Group, 1989.

Powers, William. *Living Control Systems II.* Kentucky: The Control Systems Group, 1992.

Powers, William. *Making Sense of Behavior: The Meaning of Control.* New Canaan, 1998.

Robertson, Richard J. & William T. Powers. *Introduction to Modern Psychology: The Control Theory View.* Kentucky: The Control Systems Group, 1990.

Ross, Rupert. *Dancing With a Ghost: Exploring Indian Reality.* Toronto: Reed Books Canada, 1992.

Ross, Rupert. *Returning to the Teachings.* Toronto: Penguin Books, 1996.

Senge, Peter M. *The Fifth Discipline.* New York: Doubleday, 1990.

Senge, Peter M. *The Fifth Discipline Fieldbook.* New York: Doubleday, 1994.

Senge, Peter M, C. Otto Scharmer, Joseph Jaworksi, Betty Sue Flowers. *Presence: Human Purpose and The Field of The Future.* Cambridge: The Society for Organizational Learning, 2004.

Staloch, Teri. *Implementation of Restitution, Reality Therapy and Control Theory Evaluation Project for St. Charles High School – Thesis,* Minneapolis: University of Minnesota, 2003.

Strauch, Barbara. *The Primal Teen: What the New Discoveries about the Teenage Brain Tell Us about Our Kids.* New York: Doubleday, 2003.

Thornburg, David. *The New Basics: Education and the Future of Work in the Telematic Age.* Alexandria: Association for Supervision and Curriculum Development, 2002.

Wheatley, Margaret. *Leadership and the New Science.* Berrett-Koehler Publishers Inc. 1992.

Wilson, James Q. *The Moral Sense.* New York: Macmillan, Inc., 1993.

Wolfe, Patricia. *Brain Matters: Translating Research into Classroom Practice*. Alexandria: Association for Supervision and Curriculum Development, 2001.

Video Resources
A Circle For All: Restitution Self-Discipline at École J.H. Sissons School. Quickbean Films North & *École J.H. Sissons School*, 2001.

Helping Disruptive and Unresponsive Students--Presented by Diane Chelsom Gossen. The Video Journal of Education, Volume Two, Number Six.

Restitution Staff Development Video Series, Saskatoon: Chelsom Consultants Ltd, 1994.

Restitution For Teens Video Series. Saskatoon: Chelsom Consultants Limited, 1994.

French Resources
Belair, Francine. Pour le meilleur...Jamais le pire. Montreal: Cheneliere/McGraw-Hill, 1996.

Gossen, Diane. *La réparation: pour une restructuration de la discipline a l'ecole*. Montreal: Cheneliere/McGraw-Hill, 1997.

Gossen, Diane. *La réparation: pour une restructuration de la discipline a l'ecole: guide d'animation*. Montreal: Cheneliere/McGraw-Hill, 1997.

Gossen, Diane. *Mon enfant vivre avec est une joie*. Saskatoon: Chelsom Consultants Limited, 1998.

Icelandic Translation
Gossen, Diane. Translated by Hjálmarsson, Magni. *Uppeldi til ábyrgdar: Olikar leidir, Spurt og svarad, Uppbyggingarprihornid*. Reyjavik: Islensk pyding, 2002.

Slovenian Translation
Gossen, Diane. *Restitucija: Preobrazba discipline v solah*. Radovljica: Regionalni Izobrazevalni Center, 1993

Croatian Translation
Gossen, Diane. *Restitucija: Preobrazba Skolske Discipline*. Zagreb: Alinea, 1994.

Spanish Translation
Traducio por: Allison Ann Conley, Doris Monica Diosces-Waletzsko, Jose Alonso Palacios Pacheco, *Puedes ser el propio árbitro de tus acciones*. Saskatoon: Chelsom Consultants Limited, 2004.

Diane Gossen

Diane Gossen from Saskatoon, SK has been an elementary teacher, a high school teacher, a special education teacher and the director of an alternate school for EBD students. In April 2001 Diane received the YWCA Woman of Distinction Award in the Life Time Achievement category and was a finalist for the Athena Award presented at the SABEX Awards in May 2001. She has been a Phi Delta Kappa's Gabbard Institute presenter and a speaker at the Association for Supervision and Curriculum Development Conferences in 1998 and 1999. She has presented at the Canadian Guidance and Counselors Conference, the Canadian Council for Exceptional Children Conference, the Canadian English Teachers Conference, the National Native American Bilingual Education Conference, the Learning Disabilities Association of Quebec International Conference, the Austral-Asian Cooperative Learning Conference, the Canadian Montessori Teachers Annual Conference, Institute for Reality Therapy, Control Theory and Quality Management International Conferences, the Minnesota Educators Association Conference, the North Dakota Principals Conference, and the first annual International Quality School Consortium Conference in Croatia.

Diane was on the faculty for the University of Saskatchewan 1973-75 in the Educational Curriculum Department and Graduate Studies Special Education Department. She was an assistant professor for Brandon University 1976-79. She supervised teacher training field experience component for the Gabriel Dumont Institute for First Nations teachers 1983-86. She has been an adjunct professor at LaVerne College in California and Hamline University in Minnesota. For twenty-five years she has been a senior faculty member of the Institute for Reality Therapy, Control Theory and Quality Management and the International Association for Applied Control Theory.

Diane served as the coordinator of training for the Saskatchewan Department of Justice from 1980-1981. She has been a consultant with the Saskatchewan Alcohol and Drug Abuse Commission, National Native Alcohol and Drug Commission, Saskatchewan Department of Family and Youth Services, and the Saskatchewan Young Offenders Program. She travels extensively and has presented in Canada, the United States, Australia, Japan, Ireland, Italy, Norway, Ukraine, Croatia, Slovenia and Indonesia. Most of Diane's work involves assisting districts in the school change process over several years. In the past year she has been in 72 districts in the United States. In April 2001 Diane received the YWCA Women of Distinction Award in the Lifetime Achievement category and was a finalist for the Athena Award at the SABEX Awards in May.

Diane is the author of *Restitution: Restructuring School Discipline*, the *Restitution Facilitator's Guide*, *My Child Is A Pleasure*, and the co-author of *Creating the Conditions: Leadership for Quality Schools* all of which have been translated into French. She has written and published thirty training guides for teaching self-discipline. She is featured on the *Restitution Staff Development Video Series* and the *Restitution For Teens Video Series*. The Video Journal of Education's package titled, "Dealing With Disruptive and Unresponsive Students" focuses on Diane's work in school districts in Canada and the United States. She was the creative consultant to the Canadian award winning, *Monday, Marbles and Chalk*, an eight part video series on class management. ASCD has been distributing the book *Restitution: Restructuring School Discipline* for over two years. Over 60,000 copies of this book have been sold since originally published. Phi Delta Kappa has been distributing the Restitution Staff Development Video Series.